LIES

Young Women

BELIEVE

AND THE TRUTH THAT SETS THEM FREE

LIES
Young Women
BELIEVE

AND THE TRUTH THAT SETS THEM FREE

NANCY DeMOSS WOLGEMUTH
AND DANNAH GRESH

MOODY PUBLISHERS

CHICAGO

All Scripture quotations, unless otherwise indicated, are taken from *The Holy Bible, English Standard Version.* Copyright © 2000, 2001 by Crossway Bibles, a division of Good News Publishers. Used by permission. All rights reserved.

Scripture quotations marked NKJV taken from the New King James Version®. Copyright © 1982 by Thomas Nelson. Used by permission. All rights reserved.

Scripture quotations marked NIV are taken from the *Holy Bible, New International Version*®, NIV®. Copyright © 1973, 1978, 1984, 2011 by Biblica, Inc.™ Used by permission of Zondervan. All rights reserved worldwide. www.zondervan.com. The "NIV" and "New International Version" are trademarks registered in the United States Patent and Trademark Office by Biblica, Inc.™

Italics in Scripture references indicate author emphasis.

The testimonies in this book are true. Unless both the first and last name are given, individuals' names and minor details of their stories have been changed to maintain anonymity.

Published in association with the literary agency of Wolgemuth & Associates.

Edited by Anne C. Buchanan
Interior design: Julia Ryan / DesignByJulia.com
Cover concept: Amjad Shahzad
Cover design: Erik M. Peterson
Cover photo of apple copyright © 2016 by Dimitrios Stefanidis/iStock (629734762). All rights reserved.
Images: Garden of Eden © Ng/Dreamstime; flourish © Pasko Maksim/Shutterstock; abstract flourish © Gala/Shutterstock
Back cover photo of apples on branch copyright © 2013 by Peterfactors / iStock (183434327). All rights reserved.
Author photos: Nancy DeMoss Wolgemuth — Photography by Jeff Calenberg
             Dannah Gresh — J&A Photography, Pleasant Gap, PA

Library of Congress Cataloging-in-Publication Data

Names: Wolgemuth, Nancy DeMoss, author.
Title: Lies young women believe : and the truth that sets them free / Nancy
   DeMoss Wolgemuth.
Description: Chicago : Moody Publishers, 2018. | Originally published: c2008.
   | Includes bibliographical references.
Identifiers: LCCN 2017053788 (print) | LCCN 2017054725 (ebook) | ISBN
   9780802495143 | ISBN 9780802415288
Subjects: LCSH: Teenage girls--Religious life. | Young women--Religious life.
   | Truthfulness and falsehood--Religious aspects--Christianity.
Classification: LCC BV4551.3 (ebook) | LCC BV4551.3 .D46 2018 (print) | DDC
   248.8/33--dc23
LC record available at https://lccn.loc.gov/2017053788

ISBN: 978-0-8024-1528-8

We hope you enjoy this book from Moody Publishers. Our goal is to provide high-quality, thought-provoking books and products that connect truth to your real needs and challenges. For more information on other books and products written and produced from a biblical perspective, go to www.moodypublishers.com or write to:

Moody Publishers
820 N. LaSalle Boulevard
Chicago, IL 60610

3 5 7 9 10 8 6 4 2

Printed in the United States of America

A Note to Parents and Youth Leaders

In the months of focus groups and conversations leading up to the writing of this book, we grew to love this generation of girls even more deeply. We also became increasingly aware of the depth of the deception and darkness they face. And in the decade since we originally wrote this, that darkness has only become thicker. In order to shine the light into the darkness, we felt it was necessary to be direct and specific about a variety of sensitive topics, including sexual issues, eating disorders, and occult activity.

We've tried to be discreet, without mincing words or sidestepping issues we know many young women are facing. If you have any concerns about how these subjects may be handled, please read the book prior to sharing it with your daughters or the girls in your youth group. You may also want to offer to walk through this book with them.

Thank you for your heart for these young women. We pray that the Lord will use your efforts to make an eternal difference in their lives, and that they will always love Truth and that the light of Christ will shine brightly through them to their world.

Nancy & Dannah

TABLE OF CONTENTS

✤ PART 3 • OVERCOMING LIES

INTRODUCTION

Over 1,000
young women have
taken our nationwide
BLAZING LIES TEST

Blazing Lies

We **dare** you to take a { LITTLE QUIZ }
that will **wake** you up!

From the time she was in junior high, when her parents divorced, our friend Erin Davis struggled with panic attacks. They came mostly at night and were spurred on by horrific nightmares. When she awoke, sometimes she could barely breathe. She dreaded going to sleep because she never knew when she'd wake up in the middle of the night and feel suffocated by fear. She went to college and married her high school sweetheart. Together, they ministered to the youth of their church, but Erin hid the fact that she was still plagued by panic and fear.

Worn down and completely exhausted, she finally asked some friends to pray with her about what might be causing these recurring, sudden bouts of paralyzing fear. The friends asked what kinds of thoughts ran through her mind during her panic attacks. As Erin shared what she felt during those times, it became obvious that her panic attacks were reactions to thoughts and underlying beliefs that simply weren't true. Her feelings were very real, but they were based on some pretty serious—and destructive—lies. Lies like:

Lie #1: | Everyone leaves.

Lie #2: | I have to take care of myself.

Lie #3: | I can't wear my heart on my sleeve or it'll be crushed.

It was easy for Erin's friends to see that these statements were contrary to God's Truth, but *she* needed to see it. As they prayed together, her friends asked her to consider what God would say to her about those things. Here's what she concluded.

Lie #1:   Everyone leaves.

TRUTH #1:   *"I will never leave you or forsake you."*

Lie #2:   I have to take care of myself.

TRUTH #2:   *"Be still and know that I am God."*
(Erin realized she was trying to play the role of God in her own life.)

Lie #3:   I can't wear my heart on my sleeve or it'll be crushed.

TRUTH #3:   *"They will know we are Christians by our love."*

In case you didn't catch it, the truths Erin concentrated on in that prayer time are powerful scriptures right out of the Bible. These verses became the focus for her prayer team that day. Over the next few days, she continued to meditate on those verses as she began to "reprogram" her thinking.

The results were amazing! When Erin drove home a few days later, staying in a hotel alone along the way, she slept peacefully without nightmares or panic for the first time in a long time. Her parents are still divorced. She still struggles with fear at times, but it rarely rises up as powerfully as it did night after night for almost ten years.

The lies she believed at one time put her in bondage. It was the Truth that set her free from those chains.

BONDAGE
(bon-dij) n.
slavery; the state of being bound by some external power

We believe the vast majority of Christian young women (and not-so-young women, for that matter!) are suffering the consequences of believing lies. Those consequences include broken relationships, fear, depression, and guilt, to name a few.

The results of believing a lie can be as vast as the kinds of lies there are to believe, but if there is one word that sums up the result of believing any lie it would be "bondage." The dictionary defines *bondage* as "slavery . . . the state of being bound by some external power . . . the state of being under the control of a force or influence." In other words, when you believe a lie, that lie can begin to control areas of your life.

The Bible says that "whatever overcomes a person, to that he is enslaved" (2 Peter 2:19).

Are there consuming areas of your life that you can't stop thinking about—perhaps food, guys, or your appearance?

Do you feel as if your life is being controlled by powerful emotions—like fear, depression, anger, loneliness, jealousy, or self-pity?

Are there harmful habits or destructive patterns you can identify in your life—things like cutting yourself, drinking, using drugs, or sexual activity—that you just can't seem to change or let go of?

We want you to know that you're not alone. In order to write this book, we spoke to over a thousand young women across the nation. We were looking for signs that they might be believing lies that were leading to bondage.

We didn't have to look long. Many of them readily admitted to us that they believed Satan's lies about themselves, their parents, their relationships, and even God. The twenty-five lies we address in this book come from things these young women told us. Things like: *"I'm worthless"* or *"I don't have any friends"* or *"I'll never overcome my sin."* These kinds of statements confirmed the concern that motivated us to write this book in the first place:

OUR **BLAZING LIES** TEST

Our goal in this book is to expose the Deceiver and any of his lies you may be believing. We wanted to be sure we correctly identified the issues you and your friends face. So our team hit the road to ask over 1,000 young women in ten different cities to take our nationwide **Blazing Lies** test.

About 100 of these girls took part in an informal, two-hour group discussion, which included probing questions that would reveal areas where deception was taking root. The rest participated in shorter surveys to verify what we learned from the girls we talked with face-to-face.

The result: we uncovered **25** of the most commonly believed lies among young women your age. These lies may be blazing through your life right now. We're here to douse them with some Truth!

WE HAVE BEEN LIED TO.
WE HAVE BEEN DECEIVED.

IT ALL BEGAN WITH THE FIRST WOMAN WHO EVER LIVED

Eve was approached by Satan himself, the father of all lies, in the Garden of Eden. She believed the Deceiver's lies. It's impossible to calculate all the trouble in our world that has resulted from that single event. Lies are that devastating! In fact, just one little lie can turn your world upside down.

Since that time, Satan's lies have continued to affect how all of us think. They're everywhere. They're on the pages of the magazines we read and in the movies we watch. They're all over TV and on the Internet. They can be found in the texts we get and in the conversations we have with our friends. We even begin to hear them echoing in our own thoughts, and we start lying to ourselves!

But a lot of the girls we talked to couldn't see the deception even though they were buried in the emotional, relational, physical, and spiritual consequences of those lies. That's the hard part: by their very nature, lies are deceptive; they're not easily detected. You can swallow a huge, destructive lie—hook, line, and sinker—and never even know it.

We are convinced that many young women are experiencing the destructive consequences of believing lies, but cannot see the connection between what they are experiencing and those deeply embedded lies. It makes us wonder: Can you see the deception in your own life?

THE "WHAT'S-THE-STATUS-OF-YOUR-LYING-EMBERS?" QUIZ

We dare you to take our "What's-the-status-of-your-lying-embers?" Quiz. (It's a mini-version of our nationwide Blazing Lies Test.) It should reveal—with no scientific accuracy whatsoever—areas where you might be experiencing deception. (Read: It'll give you a good idea of where there may be some embers lying around just waiting to burst into flames!)

Selecting one per pair, circle the word or set of words that reflect how you feel or respond **most** of the time.

1 **Relaxed** >>> or Totally stressed-out

2 Happy-to-be-single or **Gotta-have-a-guy**

3 Good-with-what-ya-got or **Ugly**

4 FORGIVEN OR GUILTY

5 Definitely-taking-my-problems-to-God-first or **Gotta-ask-my-friends-for-advice**

6 Got-just-enough-friends or > **LONELY**

7 **Friendly** or > Totally PMS-ing

8 AUTHENTIC **OR** HYPOCRITICAL

9 In-control-of-my-tech-world or Would-**DIE**-without-texting-and-social media

10 Confident-in-my-stand-to-be-pure or **Ashamed-to-stand-alone**

11 Content-with-what-ya-got or **MUST**-shop-now

12 The-real-deal or Different-depending-on-who-I'm-with

13 **Walking-in-victory** or Unable-to-overcome-certain-sins

14 Content-to-submit or Angry-at-my-parents

15 **Confident-of-God's-protection** or Afraid-of-Satan

OK, it doesn't take a rocket scientist to figure out we used some healthy descriptions first ("No embers here. You're a Truth speaker for your generation!") and some unhealthy descriptions last ("Lying embers alert! You're in danger!"). Which did you tend to circle?

"NO EMBERS HERE. YOU'RE A TRUTH SPEAKER FOR YOUR GENERATION."

If you live with positive, healthy emotions and relationships the majority of the time, thank God that He has kept you shielded. But don't put this book down. You may not be believing lies yourself, but you are still a part of this crisis. We need you to join us in putting out the lies that are blazing through your generation.

The Bible says we have a responsibility to try to restore those who wander off from the Truth. God wants to use *you* to reveal Truth to those who are trapped in deception. We think you'll find some practical encouragement in these pages.

"EMBER ALERT! YOU'RE IN DANGER."

We're guessing you may be in our second group. At some level, you experience negative emotions or harmful responses that are rooted in lies you've believed (though you may

THE JAMES 5 CHALLENGE

Several years ago the last two verses in the book of James jumped out at me (Nancy) during my quiet time:

If anyone among you wanders from the truth and someone brings him back, let him know that whoever brings back a sinner from his wandering will save his soul from death and will cover a multitude of sins. (James 5:19–20)

Immediately I knew why it was important for me to write a book called *Lies Women Believe: And the Truth That Sets Them Free.* I've received thousands of letters and emails from women who read that book. They shared their stories about the lies they have believed and the damage those lies have caused in their lives. In many cases, the seeds of those lies were first planted in their minds when they were teenagers—or even younger.

Many of those women have experienced newfound freedom as they have learned to counter the lies by walking in the Truth. But they earnestly wish they had known the Truth years earlier, before those lies produced so much pain. They've asked, "Isn't there something I could share with my teenage daughters, so they could learn the Truth now and wouldn't have to go through what I've been through?"

That question is what led me to team up with my friend Dannah to write this book.

not even realize they are lies). You're in the "Ember alert! You're in danger!" group. What makes us think that you are in this group? Well, we've been there. We've fallen for many of the lies on our own quiz.

However, we, along with countless others, have learned how to find freedom from the lies Satan throws our way. We want to show you how you can break free from any lies you may be believing. We want you to be free from the depression, guilt, confusion, condemnation, and discouragement that result from believing those lies.

If you don't escape from the lies, you could be facing serious danger—both immediately and down the road. We can't just stand by and watch that happen. So we're not going to beat around the bush. If you've been caught in deception, it will take nothing less than straight-up Truth to rescue you from the Deceiver.

Here's how we see the situation: Imagine we're spending the night in your home. In the middle of the night, while we're trying to sleep, we smell smoke and hear the crackle of fire. We race down the hall to find smoke rising from beneath *your* bedroom door! Without even discussing it, we would do whatever we had to do to wake you up. We wouldn't worry about whether you would be annoyed with us for waking you in the middle of the night. We would do anything to rouse you so you could get out alive!

Well, friend, we're not sleeping over, but we're here to tell you that you're in a "burning house." You're in the midst of a vast generational crisis, and lies are blazing through your world. The spiritual attack on your generation is intense. And we're going to do our best to wake you up.

What are you waiting for?
Turn the page.
LET'S PUT OUT SOME FIRES!

The Landscape of Lies

PART 1

"The devil . . . was a
murderer from the beginning,
and does not stand in the truth,
because there is no truth in him . . .
for he is a liar and the father of lies."

JOHN 8:44

The Deceiver

Where do lies come from?

Until that day, her life was almost a fairy tale—a paradise of sorts.

That all changed when Melanie was sixteen and she encountered her own personal "Tree of the Knowledge of Good and Evil." Her boyfriend was a Christian. He prayed with her. Texted her Bible verses. She'd thought she could trust him. They'd never gone that far physically. But now, he was asking for more. And she had to decide whether to give in or walk away.

He begged, *"Don't you really love me?"* His question was really an ultimatum and she knew it: *"Prove your love to me or we'll break up."*

Her boyfriend wasn't who she thought he was. That was clear, but why did she want so badly to keep him? Why was she willing to do almost anything not to lose him? Why was she even considering doing something she knew in her heart was wrong?

She found herself depressed. Stressed. Lonely. Finally, when the ache became unbearable, she reached out for advice. Her youth leader started by praying with her. After some time of talking to God, Melanie and her youth leader just sat and waited in silence.

A **NOVEL** IDEA

This book will talk a lot about Eve and how she believed the lie that took down humanity. Her story is probably familiar to you, but you'll be lost if you've forgotten what in the world the Tree of Knowledge of Good and Evil is or if you think Eve was made from Adam's big toe. (Gotcha! Are you with us?)

We have a novel idea: we'd like you to read her story for yourself. Just open your Bible to Genesis 2:15 and read through the end of chapter three. Imagine you're in the most beautiful garden ever created and sink into the drama of her story. We promise it'll read like a . . . well, a novel!

Then tears began to stream down Melanie's face. "My whole life is one big fat lie," she said.

"Tell me how," the woman asked.

She opened her eyes and spoke with certainty: "The straight A's. All my soccer trophies. A perfectly organized bedroom. Never sleeping in. Never missing devotions. My obsession with a perfect SAT score. I do that for the same reason I'm considering doing this with my boyfriend."

"Can you explain the connection?" said the woman.

As only God can, He had shown Melanie the root of her emotional confusion and distress: "I've realized that I believe I have to perform to be loved." The temptation to have sex with her boyfriend was just the fruit of a lie she had been believing. God wanted to go down deep with Melanie to rip up the root.

When I stopped striving for a moment and finally sat still, I could hear God's Truth clearly. I understood. God loves me because I'm His, not because of what I can do or how much I can excel. That night, God showed me something I couldn't see before. I realized that almost everything I did was based on this lie about performance. Seeing the truth about my value was so freeing.

REALITY READING

This book is not fiction! And we didn't want any of the stories we used to be fiction either. Though the story in this chapter is true, we've chosen not to use "Melanie's" real name. We'd do the same for you! Throughout the book, if we use only a first name, you'll know that we've changed the name.

Melanie had been lied to. Parts of her story may sound familiar to you. Or your story may be quite different. Maybe yours is a pattern of on-again, off-again friendships marked by "mean girl" moments. Constant fighting with parents who seem over-controlling. Or an ache to have your parents acknowledge that you're even alive. Secret, shameful habits. Plummeting grades. Patterns and relationships that once bothered you have come to seem "normal." But the consequences of depression, confusion, and loneliness reveal that something isn't right.

I (Nancy) received a letter one day from a young woman who had grown up in a Christian home and had been home-schooled; she even had a sense that God had a specific call on her life to serve Him. However, as her letter revealed, something wasn't right. In fact, things were very, very wrong:

🍎 *I'm having a very hard time right now. Deep depression and anger and lots of different things have changed in me. I want to end my life or hurt myself really bad, even though I feel the Lord has a special thing for me to do when I get older. I hate my life and my family. It feels like it will never end and I will have to live like this for the rest of my life. We have been to many doctors, and no one knows what is causing this.*

You'd never have guessed what was going on inside this girl by looking at her. As I read her letter, my heart ached, and I wondered how many more young women in our Christian homes and churches are experiencing similar turmoil.

If you've turned over every rock looking for physical causes to your situation, it may be that you've believed one or more lies that have become deeply embedded in your thinking and have placed you in bondage.

Let's look at how our struggle with bondage began in the first place, so we can get you on your way to freedom. To do that, let's turn our attention once again to the first woman to fall for a lie.

FEEL LIKE THERE'S
NO HOPE?

Suicide is the third leading cause of death for those aged 15 to 24.[1] We shudder to think that you may be struggling with such emotional bondage. Oh, how we wish we were there to hug you and tell you that there is hope. We're not just saying that. We mean it.

If you are struggling with thoughts of suicide, please reach out for help right now.

➡ **Cry out to the Lord.** Ask Him to rescue you from any evil influences that are trying to destroy you.

➡ **Talk to your parents, your pastor or youth pastor, or a godly Christian woman.** Ask them to pray for you and to help you get through this rough time.

➡ **Dial a help line and talk to a person live now.** We recommend calling Focus on the Family at 1-800-A-FAMILY.

THE DEFINITION OF LIES

A lie is "a false statement with deliberate intent to deceive; an inaccurate or false statement."[2] Another definition is "an impostor." A lie is an impostor of the Truth. We often don't detect lies because they camouflage themselves so well.

Back in the garden, Eve met an impostor with a diabolical agenda. He wanted Eve to become his slave by rejecting God and His purposes for her life. The serpent craftily asked, "Did God actually say, 'You shall not eat of *any* tree in the garden'?" (Genesis 3:1). That's not exactly what God had said, but it sure sounded similar. God had told Adam (and Eve) they couldn't eat from the Tree of the Knowledge of Good and Evil. Satan used a clever combination of half-truths and falsehoods *posing* as Truth.

LIE
[lahy] n.
an inaccurate or false statement; an impostor.

He began by planting doubts in Eve's mind about what God had actually said. When Eve told him that God had said they would die if they ate the fruit, he responded with a series of lies. He said, "*You will not surely die*. For God knows that when you eat of it your eyes will be opened, and *you will be like God*, knowing good and evil" (Genesis 3:4–5). He wanted her to turn her back on God, to reject His Truth, and to believe his carefully crafted lies . . . and she did.

And that's exactly what the great Impostor wants you to do too.

THE ORIGIN & PURPOSE OF LIES

The Bible tells us that Satan poses as an "angel of light" (2 Corinthians 11:14). Ezekiel 28 tells the story of how he asserted his claim to be like God. He is *the* Impostor. And his motives are malicious through and through, as Jesus Himself pointed out:

> **"The devil . . . was a murderer from the beginning,
> and does not stand in the truth, because there is no
> truth in him. When he lies, he speaks out of his own character,
> for he is a liar and the father of lies."** (John 8:44)

SATAN'S NATIVE LANGUAGE IS LYING. He speaks through different

mouthpieces, sometimes using evil rulers, false religions, social media, Netflix, popular songs, or even friends to deceive us.

Why does he lie to us? The verse above suggests that his ultimate goal is our destruction. The ultimate fruit of his lies is death. We begin to experience the results of this "death" before our hearts stop beating. Look at God's words to the first man:

> "OF THE TREE OF THE KNOWLEDGE OF GOOD AND EVIL YOU SHALL NOT EAT, FOR IN THE DAY THAT YOU EAT OF IT YOU SHALL SURELY DIE."
>
> (GENESIS 2:17)

What did God mean when He said they would die on the day they ate of the forbidden fruit? Eve clearly didn't die *physically* the day she first sinned. However, the moment she took a bite of that fruit, she did die *spiritually*—she was separated from God, who is Life.

The Tree of Life was now off-limits, and she was banished from paradise. She would now be a slave to her own sinful, selfish desires and choices. She would bear the consequences of living in a fallen, broken world, rather than enjoying the eternal pleasure of life in Paradise. She and her husband would have to endure pain and hardship as they fulfilled their basic responsibilities related to family and work. With each passing year this hardship would take its toll on their bodies, and they would eventually experience physical death.

What a vivid picture this is for us.

The moment we believe and act on a lie, as Eve did, we begin to experience consequences. We become increasingly enslaved to false, destructive ways of thinking and living. Satan's ultimate goal is our

---

THE TREE OF **KNOWLEDGE** OF GOOD & EVIL

It was the tree in the dead center of the Garden of Eden, which God had told Adam (and indirectly Eve) not to eat. They could eat of every other tree, including the Tree of Life. When Adam and Eve chose to disobey God and eat from the one tree God said was off-limits, they lost their "freedom of choice." They could no longer eat from the Tree of Life and were banned from the garden.

destruction and death. Not just physical death some day in the future. He'd like to make you a part of his walking dead on this earth, not free to enjoy God and life as He created you to live it. You see, zombies are more than the bad guys in scary movies or on Netflix. Walking around enslaved to fear and death is a very real lifestyle for many.

THE TARGET OF SATAN'S LIES

Satan targets women with his lies.

For reasons we cannot fully understand, Satan chose to target a woman for his first deception in the Garden of Eden. Twice in the New Testament the apostle Paul points out that it was the woman who was deceived: "The serpent deceived Eve by his cunning" (2 Corinthians 11:3). "Adam was not deceived, but the woman was deceived and became a transgressor" (1 Timothy 2:14).

It may feel like a bad rap, but facts are facts. Satan obviously targeted Eve, perhaps thinking that if he could get her to buy into his deception, she would influence her husband to eat the forbidden fruit with her—which is exactly what happened.

And to this day, Satan continues to target women of every age for deception.

 **Your generation is bombarded with more messages (many of them untrue) than any past generation.**

Netflix, Pinterest, texting, Instagram, Snapchat . . . The list goes on and on and is constantly changing. With so many media, the messages you are bombarded with are vastly more numerous than any previous generation has ever experienced. Never has a generation been exposed to so many messages through so many mediums.

The result is quite interesting. Social scientists have noticed that the younger generations who grew up with the Internet have responded to the information overload by becoming more careful.[3] The information available concerning the consequences of some choices has resulted in a downward trend in smoking, drinking while driving, television viewing, and even sex. You're even more likely than older generations to drink water and understand that soft drinks aren't great for you.[4]

But along with all that strength of conviction exists some of the fuzziest moral thinking that any generation has ever known. There is no longer a single source of prevailing influence or Truth. Instead, your generation tends to determine moral positions based on how a behavior makes you *feel* and whether it makes someone else *feel* good or bad. *If it makes me happy, it must be right.*

For example, 75 percent of college students admit to cheating on tests to get the grade they want. Once caught, they almost universally agree that cheating is wrong . . . unless they get away with it, in which case they believe it's OK to cheat. The technical term for this trend is "situational morality." Your generation is more likely than ours to determine right and wrong based on the context, rather than firm moral standards.[5]

The "Gender Revolution" of our day is an illustration of "morality" being impacted by how the outcome makes us feel. Your generation will be the first to mature into a gender fluid culture. That is to say, even the unmistakably clear biological distinction between male and female is no longer what people think determines gender. You can be born female, but if you identify more as male, then who's to say you're not really male?

What has brought us to this place? Stories. The stories of individuals who feel one way or another have tugged at our emotions. We have allowed stories to become authoritative because of how they make us feel. Do you see a problem with that? We sure do.

We hope you do too! Let's start a movement that will buck and begin to change the current trend of untruth! Let's start looking to the One and only source of Truth.

And let's purpose to live lives that display the power and beauty of Truth to those around us.

We're here to spur you on in that movement, by fueling you with a passion to douse Satan's lies with the Truth. Before you start, there's something you should know about *your* role in these lies.

> > > **Check out the next chapter.**

"For whatever overcomes a person, to that he is enslaved."

2 PETER 2:19

The Deceived

Where do lies get the **power** to destroy our lives?

Caitlyn was never overweight.

Not for one single day of her life. In fact, she was especially thin. And, by most standards, she was beautiful.

But the world's standards are harsh. These days the average model weighs 23 percent less than the average woman on the streets.[1] This global standard of beauty is so dangerous that Spain, Italy, and Australia have established industry guidelines requiring that runway models have a certain body mass index so they're not too thin. This mentality hasn't hit America, though. We're still killing girls in the name of a standard of beauty that cannot be attained outside of drugs and starvation. This has led two-thirds of *underweight* twelve-year-old girls to consider themselves "fat."[2]

Caitlyn was twelve when she began to believe that. At fourteen she began to do something about it. Most days she just didn't eat. She scheduled her high school classes so she wouldn't have a lunch period. If she ever caved in and ate, she ate a lot. Then she felt forced to throw up . . . and to demand a four- or five-mile run of herself.

By the time she was in high school, she'd starved herself down to eighty pounds; her period had stopped, and doctors were concerned that she'd have a

A SNAPSHOT OF EVE

Eve's name, derived from the Hebrew word *chayah* ("to live"), means "source of life." God created her when Adam was without a companion by taking a rib from Adam's side and fashioning it into a woman. Though Eve plays a notable (and notorious) role in the human story, her name occurs only four times in the Bible.

DON'T TAKE THE BAIT

If you've ever gone fishing, you know that you won't catch anything if all you do is throw an empty hook in the water. Fish are smarter than that. If you want to catch a fish, you have to put some kind of bait on your hook.

Satan's lies are the bait he uses to catch us. James 1:14–15 exposes the tactics Satan uses to ensnare us. "Each person is tempted when he is lured and enticed by his own desire. Then desire when it has conceived gives birth to sin, and sin when it is fully grown brings forth death."

Satan takes the things you desire and promises to fulfill those desires if you will simply reject God and ignore His Word. But he doesn't come right out and say, "Reject God and ignore His Word." Instead, he convinces you that doing something just once won't really hurt anything. Or that other people are finding happiness when they reject God. "And after all," he hisses, "doesn't God want you to be happy?"

When you take the bait, you've given birth to sin. Satan's goal is to use your own sin to destroy you (John 10:10). So the next time you're tempted to do something you know you shouldn't do, remember—there's a hook waiting for you. Don't take the bait.

heart attack. While she was getting treatment, she couldn't stand the weight she was gaining, though she was still considerably underweight. To punish herself, she stuck a rusty nail in her arm and left it there for days. By the time doctors discovered it, the infection had gotten so bad that they feared Caitlyn would lose her arm, if not her life.

That's not a pleasant story. But it illustrates something you need to understand: all Satan's lies are intended to destroy. This is easy to see when it comes to lies about our bodies and physical beauty. Many of them are an obvious invitation to self-destruction. And this brings us to an important and ironic Truth about his lies. They have no power. Not really. Not *without* us.

Sure, his lies are always tempting.

But that's where his power ends—*unless we cooperate*. You see, temptation can't burst into flames in your life unless you supply oxygen by believing and acting on Satan's lies. He can't take you down without your help.

Eve did a lot to help Satan in the garden. The Bible tells us that "the serpent was more crafty than any other

[lies young women believe]

beast of the field that the LORD God had made" (Genesis 3:1). Eve was in a tough place, as you have undoubtedly found yourself at times when facing temptation. But she was not a helpless victim. Satan did not *make* her sin. She *chose* to cooperate with Satan in at least four ways.

EVE COOPERATED BY LISTENING TO SATAN'S LIES

The first mistake Eve made was one you and I are still prone to make. She stuck around long enough to listen to Satan's sales pitch.

The progression to spiritual and emotional bondage begins by simply listening to something that's not true. You don't have to touch it, do it, agree with it, or even like it. You just have to be close enough to listen to the lie.

Caitlyn's battle became more intense when she began to feast on fashion magazines. One day she was an athletic middle school student, and the next she was a fashion- and beauty-obsessed girl dying from an eating disorder.

Just as Eve began her progression toward destruction by listening to a lie, Caitlyn realized that the magazines contained food for thought about guys, friendships, and social issues that interested her. She used these articles to justify the sensual photographs of half-naked young women, pro-homosexual articles, and advice on sex. She thought, *It can't hurt just to read them, right?* She cooperated with the Enemy by listening to what he had to say.

She should have run.

Eve should have run.

And you need to learn to run from anything that would send you in a direction that is contrary to God's will for your life. In fact, God's Word encourages us to do just that:

> **Flee youthful passions and pursue righteousness, faith, love, and peace, along with those who call on the Lord from a pure heart. Have nothing to do with foolish, ignorant controversies.** (2 Timothy 2:22–23)

Flee. Get away from it. Run! Eve would have done well to simply stay away from the influence of the Serpent, just as you would do well to keep your distance from every cultural voice that seeks to tempt you. Eve *knew* she was not supposed to eat from the tree, so what was she doing hanging around it?

We know we're not supposed to lie, do drugs, have sex with multiple partners, or swear. So why do so many Christians binge on Netflix series that flaunt those themes? Why do they listen to and sing popular songs with unwholesome lyrics? Why do they flock to theatres to see a movie that has "just one little sex scene"?

We know we shouldn't have idols, spend excessive money, and be obsessed with physical beauty. So why spend hours envying celebrity fashion, obsess over putting together the perfect, Pinterest-worthy outfit, and spend an hour and a half working on your hair and face every morning?

Please, oh please, don't rub up against the temptation as Eve did. Don't cooperate with Satan by getting close enough to listen to his lies.

EVE COOPERATED BY DWELLING ON LIES

After Eve listened, she began to dwell on the lies Satan had planted in her mind. Rather than running, she struck up a conversation with the Serpent; she responded to his question:

> **"We may eat of the fruit of the trees**
> **in the garden, but God said,**
> **'You shall not eat of the fruit of the tree**
> **that is in the midst of the garden,**
> **neither shall you touch it, lest you die.'"**
> (Genesis 3:2–3)

In the process, she not only distorted what God had said (we'll get to that), but she also began to dwell on what the Serpent had said.

In responding to the Serpent, Eve implied that God's restrictions were unreasonable, that He was withholding something good from them. That sounds awfully similar to what we imply when we dwell on lies rather than God's Truth. We begin to dwell on what God says we cannot have, rather than all the abundant gifts He's lavished on us.

What was the Truth?

The Truth was that God had said, "You may surely eat of every tree of the garden" (Genesis 2:16)—except one.

The Truth is that God is a generous God.

In Deuteronomy 6, Moses stressed the importance of keeping God's commandments. Then he reminded the people that the heart behind those "rules" was not to be a burden or put them in a straitjacket. God intended His laws to be for their blessing and benefit: "The LORD commanded us to do all these statutes, to fear the LORD our God, for our good always" (v. 24)!

Do you believe that God is a generous God who has given His children "every spiritual blessing in the heavenly places" (Ephesians 1:3), by giving us the gift of His Son, Jesus Christ?

Or do you choose to dwell on the boundaries He has placed in your life, forgetting that those limits are for your protection?

Do you find yourself focusing on the forbidden rather than on God's blessings?

It's easy to do. The messages you are inundated with daily tell you that "you are worth it" and "you deserve it"—as if you're not getting something you should. At the same time, they subconsciously tell you "you're not beautiful" and "you're not enough." Is it any wonder that many of us struggle with the sense of entitlement that Eve found at the base of the tree, while at the same time being overwhelmed with a deep sense of self-loathing?

We cannot afford for a minute to lose focus on God's goodness. Don't cooperate with Satan by dwelling on his lies or on the limitations rather than the blessings God has put in your life.

EVE COOPERATED BY BELIEVING LIES RATHER THAN THE TRUTH OF GOD'S WORD

By *listening* to and *dwelling* on Satan's lies, Eve began to *believe* the lies rather than what God had said. Satan led Eve to be careless with the words of God and to suggest that God had said something that He had not. God had said, "Do not *eat* the fruit of the tree." However, Eve quoted God as saying, "You shall not eat it, nor shall you *touch* it" (Genesis 3:3 NKJV).

Clearly, Eve's distortion of God's Word was a weak link in her armor to stand against Satan's enticement. After all, King David says, "I have stored up your word in my heart, that I might not sin against you" (Psalm 119:11). God's Word is an essential part of our armor against Satan's subtle attacks. Eve set herself up to sin when she dwelled on and started believing lies rather than the Truth of God's Word.

Now, this one really makes us nervous. Why? Well, can we be frank? We're concerned that a lot of you don't even *know* Scripture.

Crunch!

Didn't mean to step on your toes.

(Hey, we warned you that we were here to rescue you out of a burning house. Did you think we were going to talk about the weather?)

Most Christian teens today are too thoughtful to fall outright for alternative religions like Wicca, Buddhism, or Scientology. But many in your generation fall for something equally dangerous called *syncretism*—the fusion of two or more belief systems. For example, a teen may be a practicing Christian who utilizes New Age meditation and ancient forms of meditative Sanskrit Yoga to find peace. This is a fusion of two incompatible belief systems.

More than any other generation, you are exposed to many different worldviews through social media and the Internet. The good news is that it makes you more understanding and compassionate. The bad news is that, in general, today's teens merge Christian beliefs with opposing worldviews, often without being aware of the conflict. This can lead to potentially deadly lies infiltrating your mind and emotions.

It's so important that you listen to what God is saying to you over what the world is saying. You don't have to search mystically for His voice. He wrote it down for you! You must constantly filter everything you hear and believe through God's Word, especially if you're being exposed to the many false worldviews promoted on social media.

If your generation is going to win the battle Satan is waging against it, it will begin with *you* hiding His Word in your heart and being able to speak it accurately to those who are parroting Satan's lies in our culture. If you aren't filling your mind and heart with God's Truth, you will end up believing Satan's lies. And what you believe (not what you *say* you believe, but what you *really* believe) will determine the way that you *live*. Eve found that out the hard way.

EVE COOPERATED BY ACTING ON SATAN'S LIES
She ate the fruit.

YOU MIGHT	find yourself skipping class or grumbling at your mom.
YOU MIGHT	be prone to lying or looking at porn.
YOU MIGHT	overeat or starve yourself.

Doesn't matter how you act out; every sin in our lives begins with a lie. First, we *listen* to the lie. Then we *dwell* on it. Then we begin to *believe* it, and before long we're *acting* on it. Eventually, those sinful behaviors become a pattern in our lives and we find ourselves in *bondage*—feeling trapped by things we thought would make us happy and free.

After almost a decade, Caitlyn is still in bondage—still acting out on the lies she believes about herself. Her battle with anorexia and bulimia hasn't ended, at least not how we'd like to see it end. She's tried physicians' recommendations, years of counseling, antidepressants, and even months

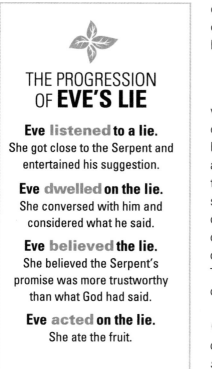

THE PROGRESSION OF **EVE'S LIE**

Eve listened to a lie.
She got close to the Serpent and entertained his suggestion.

Eve dwelled on the lie.
She conversed with him and considered what he said.

Eve believed the lie.
She believed the Serpent's promise was more trustworthy than what God had said.

Eve acted on the lie.
She ate the fruit.

of confinement in the psychiatric ward of a hospital. Nothing has helped. We believe she's missing one vital element.

TRUTH.

Kelly is another friend whose battle with anorexia has had a different outcome. One day she was seated in her counselor's office talking yet again about the depression that seemed to swallow her up on the days that she succumbed to not eating. The counselor told her she needed to stop cooperating with the lies and start choosing to saturate her mind with Truth. Kelly recalls how the light went on in her mind at that moment:

You mean I'm choosing this? I can choose to feel differently? If I spend some time retraining my mind with Truth, I might actually win this battle?

Kelly took some actions that very day that enabled her to stop cooperating with Satan's lies and to start countering those lies with the Truth. She did not experience complete victory overnight. Far from it—she had to wage a tough and long battle. At times, she still feels a pull to be overly focused on food. But she has been experiencing freedom from her eating disorder for thirteen years now!

What did she do?

What can *you* do to overcome the lies that are putting you in bondage?

>>> **We'd like to show you in the next chapter.**

"Stand therefore,
having fastened on
the belt of truth."

EPHESIANS 6:14

3

The Truth

How can I pursue **Truth**?

In 1983, the J. Paul Getty Museum in California was approached by an art dealer named Gianfranco Becchina. He had a marble statue dating from the sixth century BC. It was known as a *kouros*—a statue of a male youth. It was an extraordinary find. These kinds of statues are extremely rare and are usually damaged and fragmented. But this one was nearly perfect.

The museum began to investigate, assembling a team of experts to analyze and authenticate the piece. Core samples revealed that it was made of dolomite, an ancient marble from Greece. The surface was covered with a thin layer of calcite, which usually develops over hundreds if not thousands of years.

Researchers traced the statue's ownership back to a Swiss physician named Lauffenberger in the 1930s and a well-known Greek art dealer named Roussos before him. It seemed too good to be true, but the team agreed that this kouros was authentic, and the museum finally bought the piece for $7 million. The *New York Times* applauded the purchase, and art lovers began to travel from all over the United States to marvel.

But three people were not convinced that the statue was what it appeared to be.

Federico Zeri, who served on the museum's board of trustees, found himself observing the statue's fingernails. Something seemed wrong. Evelyn Harrison, an expert on Greek sculpture, had "a hunch" that something wasn't right the moment she first saw the statue. Thomas Hoving, the former director of the Metropolitan Museum of Art in New York, said the first word that came to his mind was "fresh." And "fresh" isn't a word you'd use to describe a 2,600-year-old statue. This fringe group put pressure on the museum to dig deeper.

Bit by bit, the truth began to unfold. Lawyers traced the documents and found that one of the letters dated 1952 had a postal code that didn't exist until twenty years later. Another referred to a bank account that wasn't opened until almost ten years later. Greek art analysts determined that the feet were definitely modern and British, not ancient and Greek. It was discovered that the calcite on the surface had been created by soaking the marble statue in potato mold for a few months.

As it turned out, the museum had acquired a fake—an "impostor" from a forger's workshop in Rome—that dated to the early 1980s. The truth had been protected by three people who stood firm in their knowledge of art and refused to be caught up in the enthusiasm of the crowd.

This story is a powerful picture for us as Christians. The path of least resistance is to go with the flow and follow the crowd, without stopping to ask, "Is this really true?" Those who love Christ and stand for Truth will always be a small minority. We are called to stand firm for that Truth, regardless of how few people may agree with us.

THE **LITMUS** **TEST** FOR TRUTH

God knew how challenging it was going to be to distinguish between the Truth and a cleverly disguised lie. So He didn't leave anything to our imagination. John 8:31–32 (NIV) says, "If you hold to my teaching, you are really my disciples. Then you will know the truth, and the truth will set you free."

This takes us back to the Word of God. If we listen to the Truth, dwell on it, believe it, and act on it, that Truth will set us free.

Stand therefore, having fastened on the belt of truth, and having put on the breastplate of righteousness. (Ephesians 6:14)

How do you learn to stand? The same way Zeri, Harrison, and Hoving did. You become so familiar with the Truth that when an impostor shows up you can quickly discern that it's a counterfeit.

YOU STUDY TRUTH

It's not enough to know that the source of lies is Satan or even to realize how you have cooperated with him to empower lies. You've got to become familiar and saturated with Truth.

THE DEFINITION OF TRUTH

As we were writing this book, we asked over two hundred Christian young women to write a definition of *lie* and one for *Truth*. Most were perplexed. Of those who took a stab, most of their definitions were simply statements of opposites: "a lie is something that is not true"; "Truth is something that is not a lie."

The problem with these "definitions" is that they use circular reasoning. There's not a foundational starting point for the definition of either a lie or the Truth. Indulge us for a moment if we seem to be too basic. We want to get this right!

> ## TRUTH
> [trooth] n.
> *agreement with a standard or original;*
> *Jesus Christ.*

You'll recall that in an earlier chapter we noted that a lie is "an impostor." Dictionary.com says that Truth is "agreement with a standard or original."[1] The Getty Museum staff discovered the truth about their $7 million statue by holding it up to the standard of an original kouros. So we must bring every thought and act into agreement with a "standard or original." The question is: What is our standard for Truth? What is the "original" that defines Truth?

THE SOURCE OF TRUTH

The standard or original for Truth is Jesus Christ. Few Christians grasp this foundational fact. Of the hundreds of Christian young women we asked to define Truth, only *one* wrote:

Truth is Jesus Christ and His Word.

Jesus Himself said, "*I am* the way, and *the truth,* and the life" (John 14:6). He is the definition of Truth. He is the perfect standard; He determines what is right and good and true. Jesus reveals the Truth to us. He does this through the written Word of God—the Bible! In fact, "the Word" is actually one of Jesus' names (John 1:14).

If Jesus reveals Truth for us through His written Word, how do we use that to combat the lies that are thrown at us? Well, this brings us back to our friend Kelly, who overcame the lies she believed about her body and stopped using anorexia and bulimia to act upon those lies. You'll recall that she has been free from that bondage for many years. How did she do it?

She turned to Christ and His Word. She found verses that countered the lies she had believed. She wrote those verses out and posted them in her room, in her car, in her textbooks—anywhere she could staple, tape, or glue them. Whenever her mind or her emotions were assaulted with lies, she would read those verses aloud. Gradually, her thinking began to change as her mind was renewed with the Truth.

🍎 *I didn't feel different immediately, but I knew that I finally had a weapon. I slowly began to believe what I was reading aloud more than the lies I once felt so powerfully.*

GOD
CANNOT LIE

It may be hard to imagine that there is something God cannot do, but it's a fact. Numbers 23:19 says, "God is not man, that he should lie." Titus 1:2 also affirms that He does not lie. He can't. It is the antithesis of who He is because He is Truth.

What a comfort this can be as we search His Word and find that He is "enthralled by [our] beauty" (Psalm 45:11 NIV) or that He "will not leave" us (Deuteronomy 31:6) or that nothing can ever separate us from His love (Romans 8:39). No matter what our emotions or circumstances may tell us, we can believe His Word!

Are your emotions or your circumstances currently causing you to believe any lies? Can you think of a verse in the Bible that reveals the Truth about your situation?

Kelly moved from the bondage of thinking about food every day all day long and being bombarded with lies about her value and beauty, to believing the Truth and being free to act accordingly.

[lies young women believe]

I knew I was free when one day a friend shared with me how she didn't think she could overcome her eating disorder because she could never stop thinking about it. That used to be me. But that day, I realized I hadn't thought about it for months. I was free.

TRUTH SETS YOU FREE

There are consequences to believing lies. Those consequences may include depression, problems in relationships, or hopelessness. There are also results to believing Truth. Jesus promises that you and I can know Truth and that "the truth will set [us] free" (John 8:32). Kelly and countless others have experienced this freedom; now it's your turn.

Will it be easy?

No. As we said earlier, you'll be in the minority. You'll need to stand against the crowd. That's why you need to decide early in life whether you're going to go with the crowd or stand for Truth. The way you are living your life *now* is establishing a pattern for compromise or for walking in Truth. Decisions you make today will have long-term implications. It can be difficult up front to base your life on the Truth, but if you do, you will reap the benefits for the rest of your life.

> > > Now, let's begin to dismantle twenty-five of the lies young women acknowledged they are falling for. Let's start to stand for Truth!

Lies Young Women Believe

PART 2

"All your words are true;
all your righteous laws
are eternal."

(PSALM 119:160)

Shelly

I hate God because people at church tell me God is like my father. You have no idea what my father is like and what he has done to me. If God is like that then . . . no way! 😠

Maybe I can't understand completely but for me, I cannot relate to God in the way I relate to my dad. My relationship with my dad hasn't been good for the past few years. I think of God as completely separate from my dad. God is a perfect dad that won't mess up like my biological father has. In a way I think of God as Father, but not like MY father.

"What comes into our minds when we think about God is the most important thing about us."

A. W. TOZER

Lies about God

Buckle up! Here come 25 lies young women believe. But first . . .

. . .A FEW GROUND RULES

1 **Don't expect to find answers to all of your life's problems.** This list isn't exhaustive. Satan is a master Deceiver. His lies are endless. Our goal is simply to address some of the lies most commonly believed by Christian young women today. In the last section of this book, we'll teach you how to tackle the ones we missed.

2 **Don't expect a step-by-step guide to overcoming the lies that plague you.** We will not address any of these lies thoroughly. Entire books have been written on many of these subjects. Our goal is just to give you a broad overview of the kinds of things that can be destructive in your life. (Check out the LiesYoungWomenBelieve.com blog for more help on lots of these topics and for daily doses of Truth!)

3 **Do expect to be stretched.** Your first response to some of these lies may be, "I don't believe that!" However, what we really believe is revealed not by what we say, but by how we *live*. You see, just because you *know* Truth doesn't mean you *believe* it. You need to ask yourself, "Do I live as though I believe this lie?"

4 **Do use your Bible.** Don't just take our word (or anyone else's) for what's true. You may find yourself disagreeing with us at points. The issue isn't really what we think (or what *you* think), but what *God* thinks! Learn to examine and evaluate everything through the grid of His Word. Take time to look up Scripture references we've included—you may even want to write them out in your journal. It'll help you get supersaturated with Truth.

5 Do interact with others. This is so important that we've even written a *Lies Young Women Believe Study Guide* to make it easier. We witnessed young women participating in our focus groups who thought they were the only one battling a particular issue. As they interacted with others, they learned they were not alone. We want the same for you. As you explore these themes with others through the Study Guide, you'll experience the power of godly friendships to help you walk through this life in Truth.

Let's start by looking at the lies young women believe about God. Nothing is more crucial than this. If you have wrong thinking about God, you will have wrong thinking about everything else. What you believe about God will determine the way you live. If you believe things about Him that aren't true, you will eventually act on those lies and end up in bondage.

#1 { "God is not enough." }

Right out of the gate, the vast majority of our focus group respondents admitted that they agreed with the statement "God is not enough." In fact, we were a little shocked that so many *consciously* believed this lie. Many of the things that were shared triggered an awareness of this lie. Girls admitted thinking things like:

"IF ONLY	my parents could stay together, *that* would be enough."
"IF ONLY	I could find one good friend, *that* would be enough."
"IF ONLY	I would be valedictorian, *that* would be enough."
"IF ONLY	I got on the track team, *that* would be enough."

One thing bubbled to the top of the conversation consistently and, though we'll devote a lot more attention to this in a future chapter, we need to mention it here. The main thing that rivals God for being enough: friends. Many believed that they needed their friends more than God. Most acknowledged that if they have a problem or need advice about something, they are more likely to text or call a friend than to talk to God about it.

 A lot of times when I pray, I feel like I can hear God, but it is not the same as the direct response that I get from my friends.

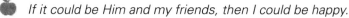 *Instead of talking to God first, sometimes I talk to my friends because I know I will get an immediate response and that they will take my side.*

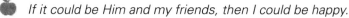 *If it could be Him and my friends, then I could be happy.*

Sounds pretty out of order, doesn't it? The good news is that most who believed this lie knew it was an area where their conduct exposed what they really believed.

Nothing less than God can ever fill the part of our heart that was created for God. It took me (Nancy) many years to start to grasp this basic Truth. As a teen and into my young adult years, I tended to look to other people to fill my emotional tank. But I could never get enough—I always craved "more." And when the people I counted on dropped out of the picture for whatever reason, I was miserable (and made others miserable!).

When I was thirty, a close friend and mentor died; another moved away, and a third friend was removed from my life through a tragic circumstance. I was devastated. For the next several months, I struggled with feelings of disappointment with God and battled some intense doubts about my faith.

Finally, as I began to cry out to the Lord, He showed me that I had been

I NEED MY **FRIENDS** MORE THAN **GOD**

We asked young women to respond to the statement "God is not enough to satisfy."

Always or sometimes agree ... 88%

Never agree 12%

Most reported that they couldn't live without friends and that they turn to friends before God. Material things ranked a distant second.

looking to my friends to meet my needs and to fill the deepest places of my heart. I discovered that by putting people in the place of God, they had become *idols* in my life. I began to realize that there was no human (or anything else) on the planet that could truly satisfy my unfulfilled longings. I discovered that I was insecure because I was placing my trust in people, who could be taken away from me, rather than in the One who never changes and who will never leave me.

That desperate season proved to be a huge turning point in my life. I repented of my idolatry and asked God to show me when I was expecting others to meet needs that only He could meet. He brought me to the place where I could honestly say:

WHOM HAVE I IN HEAVEN BUT YOU?
AND THERE IS NOTHING ON EARTH THAT I
DESIRE BESIDES YOU. (PSALM 73:25)

God is enough; He will meet your needs and wants to be your closest confidant. His Word promises: "And my God will supply every need of yours according to his riches in glory in Christ Jesus" (Philippians 4:19). He is the One who can heal your heart when it is broken (Psalm 147:3).

HE IS THE ONE who can encourage, guide, and protect you (Psalm 121:7).
HE IS THE ONE who can make you feel safe when others fail you (Psalm 27:10).
HE IS THE ONE who can make you feel valued no matter what you can or cannot do (Matthew 10:29–21).

We get to know our friends better as we spend time with them. The same is true about having a friendship with God. As we spend time reading and thinking about what He's saying to us in His Word, or as we pray or meet with others to worship Him or study the Bible together, our relationship with Him grows deeper. The more you get to know God, the more you see that He is the only One who can meet your deepest needs.

There's nothing wrong with having friends, a 4.0 GPA, athletic ability, nice clothes, or a happy, healthy family—God may bless us with all those gifts and more. But none of those things can satisfy the deepest longings of our hearts; and those gifts are really only meaningful when our relationship with Him is at the center of our lives.

#2 { "God is not really involved in my life." }

Oxford University Press released a landmark study that analyzed the spiritual lives of American teenagers. They found that, among those teens who claim to believe in God, their belief would best be described as a form of deism.[1] They believe God exists and that He created the world, but they think He now stands aloof from it. We really hoped our Christian young women would disagree, but they didn't. The majority tended to feel that God was not really involved in their lives. Here's how one put it:

 God is so big. He has so much to take care of with wars and natural disasters and stuff like that. I find it hard to believe that He cares about what is going on in my life.

STOP AND THINK ABOUT THAT FOR A MINUTE. You say you

believe in the God of the universe who is all-powerful and all-knowing; but you also think He is unaware of or unconcerned with the details of your life? Listen to what Jesus had to say:

Are not five sparrows sold for two pennies? And not one of them is forgotten before God. Why, even the hairs of your head are all numbered. Fear not; you are of more value than many sparrows. (Luke 12:6–7)

We are worth much more than a sparrow, and He even sees when each sparrow falls to the ground. He promises that His eyes are on you and that He hears your cries (Psalm 34:15). You are valuable to God, and He knows and cares about the details of your life!

I (Dannah) have found God to be involved in the most minute details of my life, proving His faithfulness and love again and again. A few years ago my husband and I led a group of people to Zambia, Africa. Nervous about being responsible for twenty-nine people in a Third World nation where the medical care was inadequate, I pleaded with God before we left to keep everyone healthy and to somehow provide anything I might have forgotten to pack.

IMMANUEL

This name of God reminds us that God is intimately involved in our lives. "El" means God. The first part of the name means "with us." God is the "with us God."

On our first night there, my husband, Bob, was stricken with a terrible bloody nose. I had never seen such a gusher! We spent most of the night packing his nose and praying that the bleeding would stop. Nine hours later, it still had not, and we had resigned ourselves to the fact that a visit to the local hospital would be necessary to cauterize the artery. We collected his passport and other paperwork, and my Zambian friends were about to take him. I pleaded one more time, "Lord, can You please avert this visit to the hospital?"

Just then, our dear friend James Brown popped out of his dormitory.

"Hey, I heard Bob has a bloody nose," he hollered in his thick southern drawl.

"Yes, we're sending him to the hospital," I answered as we continued to walk toward the car that was waiting.

"Don't do that," he said, walking toward us and waving a small packet in the air. "I had the same thing last week. The doctor at the ER sent me here with a couple of nose cauterization kits just in case. We can do it here."

God cared enough about Bob and me to prompt our friend to pack exactly what we needed!

He cares about you that much too.

Perhaps it is not that God is distant from you, but that you are distant from God. James 4:8 invites us to "draw near to God, and he will draw near to you. Cleanse your hands, you sinners, and purify your hearts, you double-minded." How long has it been since you took time to draw near to God, and realized that He is always near to you? It is double-minded to believe that God exists but He is not involved in your life.

SPEAKING OF DOUBLE-MINDED, CHECK OUT THIS NEXT LIE.

#3 { "God should fix my problems." }

It's ironic that this lie is embraced by so many young women, since you are also likely to believe that "God isn't really involved in my life." How can both be true?

Most of the young women we spoke to said they knew in their heads that they should not expect God to fix their problems, but readily admitted that their actions demonstrated an unholy belief that He should. Here's how one young woman summed it up:

🍎 *I know that I am not supposed to believe that God should fix my problems, but a lot of times as Christians, that is how we think. Most people, if they don't have a regular habit of praying, that's when they go to God . . . when they need Him to fix a problem.*

Even many Christians who *do* have a regular habit of praying tend to simply offer God a "to-do" list rather than enjoying a balanced prayer life that includes praise, thanksgiving, listening, and confession. This kind of thinking reduces God to a cosmic genie who exists to please and serve us. It suggests that the goal in life is to be free from all problems—to get rid of everything that is difficult or unpleasant.

God is more concerned about changing us and glorifying Himself than about solving all our immediate problems (Romans 8:29). That doesn't mean God doesn't care about the things that matter to us. He's not just sitting up in heaven waiting to see if we'll manage to survive. No, the God of the Bible is "a very present help in trouble" (Psalm 46:1). However, He's also concerned with using our problems to shape us and to make us like His Son, Jesus. Scripture tells us that we are to learn "obedience through what he suffered" (Hebrews 5:8), and that God uses hardship in our lives to draw us closer to Himself and make us more responsive and obedient to Him.

HOW **TEENS** PRAY

Most teens who pray regularly admit that the majority of their prayer time is spent petitioning God.

77% commonly pray for a sick friend or relative

72% petition God for personal needs

71% pray for global concerns

23% ask for material things [2]

Prayer is meant to be a two-way communion with God. It should include hearing from Him, praising Him, thanking Him, waiting on Him, contemplating His Word, and letting Him know our needs. If your prayer life is mostly made up of personal requests, maybe you believe the lie that "God should fix my problems."

In fact, the Bible teaches us that God uses trials and difficult times in our lives to help us grow. James 1:2–4 says that we are to be joyful in our trials, because God is testing our faith so that our faith will grow stronger. And Romans 5:3–4 tells us that "suffering produces endurance, and endurance produces character, and character produces hope." So even in our trials and our suffering, God is at work in our lives!

Some of you offered good advice about the importance of submitting to the suffering God permits in our lives:

 It's okay to ask God to fix your problems, but you need to look beyond the problem and realize that maybe God's trying to teach you something through that problem.

 You have to really humble yourself and submit to His will. Put yourself aside and say, "Whatever you ask, Lord."

THE FOCUS OF OUR PRAYER LIFE SHOULD NOT BE "GOD, THIS IS WHAT I WANT" BUT "GOD, WHAT DO YOU WANT OF ME?"

In our goal to become like Christ, we should pray the way He prayed. In His moment of greatest trial, Jesus pleaded, "My Father, if it be possible, let this cup pass from me; nevertheless, not as I will, but as you will" (Matthew 26:39). We don't often hear prayers that reflect this kind of submission and obedience, but we are called to follow Christ's example.

I (Nancy) experienced my first major test in this area on the weekend of my twenty-first birthday. I'd spent the weekend at home visiting my parents and six brothers and sisters. On Saturday afternoon, my parents took me to the airport to catch a flight back to Virginia, where I was serving on the staff of a local church. My dad was planning to play tennis with some friends later that day, so he was wearing his tennis clothes when he dropped me off. It would be the last time I would see him here on this earth.

When I landed at the other end, a family I knew met me at the airport. They told me my mother was trying to reach me (no cellphones back then!). When I called her back, she told me that my dad had suffered a heart attack on the tennis court and had died before he hit the ground. He was with the Lord.

It was hard to believe. He was just fifty-three years old; my mother was only forty. With no warning, she was now a widow with seven children, ages eight to twenty-one. My dad had a fervent heart for God and was actively involved in ministry. My brothers and sisters and I adored him; we admired his wisdom and example as a dad. We would never have another chance to sit around the dinner table and talk with him; he would not be there to counsel us as we made major life decisions; he would not attend any of his children's weddings or hold any of his grandchildren in his arms.

[lies young women believe]

Yet within moments of hearing the news that he was gone, the Lord brought to mind a paraphrase of a verse I had read just days earlier: *"God is good, and everything he does is good"* (Psalm 119:68). In the wake of that enormous loss, God graciously reminded me of something my dad had spent many years teaching us—that God can be trusted, even in the midst of tragedy. For sure, death was not part of God's original plan for the human race. But He is a good, redeeming God who is making all things new.

And in that moment, He assured my heart that my dad's death was not an "accident" or a mistake, but that it was part of a larger, greater plan, and that ultimately He would use this heartbreaking loss to bring glory to Himself and to help me (and others) become more like Jesus.

I look back and am so grateful for a dad who taught me to trust God's choices, rather than insisting that He keep me from ever experiencing pain, or that He solve all my problems. What a great gift he left me.

That brings us to an important topic: dads. Maybe you haven't had the same kind of experience that I've had with my dad. Let's talk about what that might do to your perception of God.

#4 { "God is just like my father." }

I (Dannah) facilitate events for teens around the nation. A few years ago, the Lord prompted me to add a session on fathers to the events. I'd heard so many stories of fatherlessness, and I felt teens needed a place to face the hurt and to start the process of forgiving their dads. I wasn't prepared for the volume of emotions and tears that surfaced. I heard stories like these:

My father did unspeakable things to my sister. All the while, he completely ignored me. She was his pet. I was his burden. Eventually he died, and my mom didn't want us. We were passed from foster home to foster home until we were adopted. The social workers label me as having an attachment disorder. I'd say I just had a really lousy dad, and that takes some time to heal from.

My relationship with my dad hasn't been so good for the past few years. I used to be "his girl," but now he's distant and I don't know what I've done wrong. I cannot relate to God the way I relate to my dad, or we wouldn't relate at all.

If you have been wounded by a father—or another man you trusted—you may find it difficult to trust God. You may even be afraid of Him or angry with Him. The thought of responding to Him as a Father may be repulsive to you. And yet, Jesus freely called God His Father and instructed His disciples to address Him as their Father. Paul invites believers to call God "Abba," which means "Daddy" (Romans 8:15).

GOD IS A FATHER, BUT HE IS NOT LIKE ANY MAN YOU HAVE EVER KNOWN.

The wisest, kindest earthly father is only a pale reflection of our heavenly Father. The God of the Bible is infinitely more wonderful and pure and loving than even the most wonderful father. God our Father is perfect (Matthew 5:48) and unchanging (James 1:17). Our earthly fathers cannot be those things (Matthew 7:11). Regardless of how you may think or feel, God is a good Father who dearly loves His children—including you. He can be trusted.

LEARN TO RELATE TO YOUR EARTHLY FATHER THROUGH GOD rather than relating to God through your earthly father.

We really have it backwards. Some of the power in this lie comes from trying to attach fatherlike qualities to God when we should be asking God how to respond to our earthly fathers.

God requires you to "honor your father" (Ephesians 6:2). He doesn't say to honor him if he's a good dad. He doesn't say to honor him until you are eighteen. He simply says to honor him. Period.

Having said that, we realize there are some cases where this can be really difficult. Your dad may have wronged you in some pretty serious ways. But God calls us to forgive those who sin against us (Luke 11:4). Choosing to forgive may feel impossible, especially when you're dealing with someone who has failed to protect and cherish you as a father should. However, God's Word asks us to forgive our offenders, not because they deserve it, but because Christ has forgiven *us* of so much.

No matter how deeply your father may have wounded you, you will find freedom and hope as you choose to forgive him. We aren't suggesting that it's easy or that it'll offer you a quick fix. Forgiveness and healing may involve a long, hard journey, but God will help you every step of the way.

Callie forgave her father years before she began to experience any direct benefits (other than a clean heart).

My dad left when I was a baby. I never saw him until I was a teenager, and then he let it be known that he didn't really know me and didn't really want to know me. All my dreams of who he might be were shattered, and I had to begin the journey to forgive him. There weren't any rewards from it. I just did it. It freed me.

It wasn't until I was out of college one year ago that my dad finally decided to try. It's still a tender relationship, but I know God is giving it to me because I spent eight years on a mission to experience forgiveness.

Why not try choosing to forgive *your* dad? Then, begin to move back toward him by making a deliberate attempt to overlook his human frailties and choosing instead to admire any strengths he might have, such as his protection, strength, or provision. This could heal your relationship with your dad and enable you to begin to view God in a more truthful light.*

By the way, you never know how much (or how little) time you may have with your parents. About a week before my (Nancy's) dad died, he called and expressed that he would really like for me to come home to celebrate my twenty-first birthday with the family. I struggled with the decision—I had been with the family on vacation a couple weeks earlier, and weekends were a busy time in my job. He didn't tell me I *had* to come home, but as I thought about it, I felt that I should honor my dad's request.

I'm so thankful I did. Our entire family was together that weekend for the first time in eighteen months. As it turned out, it would also be the last time we'd all be together before his death.

All these lies about God are best remedied by the same thing: STUDY THE BIBLE TO GET TO KNOW JESUS, who is the "radiance of the glory of God and the exact imprint of his nature" (Hebrews 1:3). When you see Christ as He is, it will be harder to believe things about God that aren't true.

* Please talk with a wise, older friend, pastor, or counselor if it is not possible or you feel it would be inappropriate for you to "move back toward" your father—for example, if he has never been in your life or has been been physically or sexually abusive.

DOUSING LIES WITH THE TRUTH

the lie

the truth

God is not enough.

• Friends can never fill the part of your heart that was created for God. Psalm 73:25

• God is enough; He will meet your needs and wants to be your closest confidant. Psalm 40:4; Job 42:2

God is not really involved in my life.

• You are valuable to God, and He cares about the details of your life. Psalm 34:15

• Draw near to God, and He will draw near to you. James 4:8

God should fix my problems.

• God is more concerned with changing you than fixing all your problems. Hebrews 5:8; James 1:2–4; Romans 5:3–4

• The focus of your prayer life should not be "what do I want," but "what does God want." Matthew 6:33; 26:39

God is just like my father.

• God is a father, but He is unlike any man you have ever known. Matthew 5:48; 7:11; James 1:17

• Learn to relate to your earthly father through God rather than God through your earthly father. Ephesians 6:2; Luke 6:37; Exodus 34:6–7

[lies young women believe]

making it personal

THE MOST IMPORTANT PART OF THIS BOOK IS HOW YOU APPLY IT.

We'd love to hear that you've filled a journal with key thoughts and verses about what God has taught you. Why not begin today by writing a journal entry that answers these questions:

What lies have I been most likely to believe about God?

What Scripture verses can I store in my heart to help me counter those lies with the Truth?

Daisy

Check out the weird picture on Josh's Instagram feed. Freaky EVIL! Satan has to be EVERYWHERE!

What?!?!

Why else do I feel like he influences me? Like he is in my head confusing my thoughts and I have to try to decipher if it is God or something else . . .

God is sooooooo much bigger than Satan and only God has the power to be everywhere at once.

but why do I feel like Satan is EVERYWHERE?!

maybe that is why he is called a deceiver

"Enemy-occupied territory—
that is what this world is.
Christianity is the story of how
the rightful king has landed . . .
and is calling us all to take part in
a great campaign in sabotage."

C. S. LEWIS

Lies about Satan

One of my (Dannah's) closest friends is Brendah Maseka. She lives in Zambia, Africa. She has grown up with a keen awareness of demonic forces and has witnessed many incidents when they have been cast out of people. As she walks to the school where she works, she often passes by the witch doctor's house, and on occasion she sees people "slithering like snakes. It is as if they have no bones in their bodies. It's not something someone could fake." She says that even those who are not believers have seen demonic activities. In her words: "It's just how it is in Africa."

Brendah has an "ancestral name" that her father gave her when she was born. She won't tell me what it is. She won't even allude to what it means. We have shared the deepest, darkest secrets of our lives, but she won't tell me what I perceived to be "just" a name. To her, it's not "just" a name. She is all too familiar with the power of Satan and is quite content with fleeing from it to the point of saying nothing that might glorify him—including repeating her ancestral name.

In talking with teen women across the nation, we were concerned that many times their sense of who Satan is and their response to him does, in fact, glorify him. That is, it shines a spotlight on him and overestimates his power. On the other hand, some girls we spoke to vastly underestimated him. We found a great deal of confusion about who Satan is and what he can do.

"HE IS EVERYWHERE."
"He can hear my thoughts."
"He isn't even real."

We can understand why there's confusion. In a recent survey, more than half of Americans said they believe that Satan is only a symbol of evil as opposed to a literal being.[1] This faulty belief finds us ill-equipped to disciple one another in how to respond to Satan. Many in your generation are oblivious to Satan's presence and influence. And those who do believe he is a literal being risk having an overblown sense of his power.

You need to have a basic understanding of who Satan is and how he operates. Let's see if we can set the record straight. Then we'll deal with a couple of the most prominent lies you believe related to Satan and his supernatural war against our holy God.

WHO IS SATAN?

Satan was a beautiful archangel—one of the chief angels—who was kicked out of heaven for aspiring to be like God. The prophet Ezekiel gives a vivid description that most Bible scholars agree refers to Satan. He writes that originally Satan was:

"the seal of perfection" (NKJV)

> **"full of wisdom"**
>> **"perfect in beauty"**
>>> the **"guardian cherub"**

But then, records Ezekiel, Satan became:

"filled with violence"

> **"proud because of [his] beauty"**
>> **"corrupted"** in **"wisdom"** (Ezekiel 28:12–17)

As a result of his arrogance and rebellion, God cast him out of heaven. Satan thought he could make himself "like the Most High" (Isaiah 14:14). But he is nothing like God. For starters, Satan had a beginning, and one day there will be an end to his reign over this world when he'll be thrown into "the lake of fire" and tormented forever and ever (Revelation 20:10). God has no beginning, and His reign will never end.

WHAT CAN'T HE DO?

Satan's power is drastically different from God's. God is all-powerful (omnipotent) and all-knowing (omniscient); He is also present everywhere (omnipresent). Satan has divinely appointed limitations.

HE'S NOT OMNISCIENT (all-knowing). The Bible tells us that he doesn't know when Christ will return (Matthew 24:36). We can assume that there are many other things he does not know.

HE'S NOT OMNIPOTENT (all-powerful). His power is limited and subordinate to God (see Job 1:12; 2:6; Luke 22:31; James 4:7; Matthew 4:1–11;

[lies young women believe]

Ephesians 6:16). He cannot do anything without permission from God.[2]

HE'S NOT OMNIPRESENT (present everywhere at once). He must rely on the angels who followed him in his rebellion, and are now demons, to be everywhere he wants to be.[3]

The Bible describes Satan as our adversary, our accuser, our tempter, and the deceiver. He is described as "a roaring lion, seeking someone to devour" (1 Peter 5:8). Even though he is limited, with God's permission, Satan can and often does make life difficult for us. This seems to be where the confusion begins, so let's look at the first lie we unveiled that many Christian teens believe about Satan.

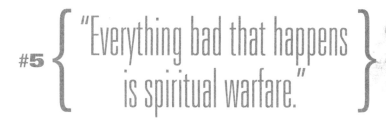

#5 { "Everything bad that happens is spiritual warfare." }

We heard this lie expressed in different ways by young women in our focus groups.

I think that when bad things happen, it is Satan testing God.

He is real because when bad things happen it is Satan and God fighting.

It is true there is a battle going on that involves Satan and his evil forces. The Bible makes it clear that we are involved in that spiritual battle:

> **For we do not wrestle against flesh and blood, but against the rulers, against the authorities, against the cosmic powers over this present darkness, against the spiritual forces of evil in the heavenly places.** (Ephesians 6:12)

Sometimes the bad things that happen to us are a direct assault from Satan. At times, we both have experienced unusually fearful thoughts, intense temptation, or a crippling sense of inadequacy when we were preparing to minister to others. We believe those can be initiated by Satan. At such times, it is appropriate to ask God to "deliver us from the evil one" (Matthew 6:13 NIV). But not all the bad things that happen to us are direct, undeserved assaults from Satan and his minions. Satan is not the only enemy of our soul.

Many bad things that happen are brought on by our own choices. One of the greatest opponents to your Christian growth is *you*—what the New Testament often refers to as the "flesh" (see Romans 7:25; Galatians 5:16; 1 Peter 2:11). For example, when you arrive for your first day of college you'll be greeted by numerous credit card companies. All of them will have "free" gifts for you if you sign up for their card. You could be tempted by the cozy collegiate blanket for home games, the month of free pizza, *and* the $25 iTunes gift card.

Don't fall for it! If you do, by the time you get out of college, you're likely to have racked up major debt. In fact, researchers predict that many of you will still be working to pay off that debt in your seventies.[4] Talk about a trap!

If you use credit cards to purchase items you can't afford, sooner or later you will find yourself in financial bondage. When you're discouraged because you can't pay your bills, it's not because Satan has attacked you. It's because you've made unwise choices. You've been your own enemy.

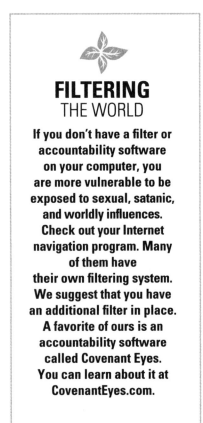

FILTERING
THE WORLD

If you don't have a filter or accountability software on your computer, you are more vulnerable to be exposed to sexual, satanic, and worldly influences. Check out your Internet navigation program. Many of them have their own filtering system. We suggest that you have an additional filter in place. A favorite of ours is an accountability software called Covenant Eyes. You can learn about it at CovenantEyes.com.

Sometimes the bad things that happen are brought on by the influence of the fallen world in which we live. The New Testament uses the Greek word *kosmos* to refer to the "order" or "system of organized culture apart from God" (John 15:18–19; 1 Corinthians 1:18–24). This "kosmos" attacks our appetites and our eyes and feeds our pride. That world system is as great an enemy today as it has ever been.

For example, pornography wasn't a major issue for most people in our grandparents' generation. They had to go to seedy places to find it. It's a huge problem today because it's everywhere. You can hardly drive through any city without being assaulted by sexual images on billboards. You can be on the Internet to buy something as innocuous as a strand of pearls and find yourself inadvertently viewing vile pictures if your online viewing isn't filtered. According to one study, 90 percent of sixteen- to eighteen-year-olds have viewed pornography online, most of them while doing homework.[5]

If that happened to you, you probably weren't looking for it. But neither does it necessarily mean that Satan planned an attack specifically for you. It means that you will sometimes face sinful things simply because you live in a fallen world.

When we face hard times, we shouldn't automatically assume the source is Satan. The Bible is clear that our battle for holiness is waged on three fronts. We battle Satan; but we also battle our own flesh and the world. We cannot ignore any of these three areas. In fact, they are often intertwined— and in some sense, Satan is involved in all of them. But when bad things happen, you can't just cry "spiritual warfare" as if you weren't responsible.

Even if he is the source of your problems, you still have personal responsibility. If you are subjected to demonic influence or oppression, remember that God has given you through Christ and the cross everything you need for freedom. That is why repentance, confession, and the acceptance of biblical Truth are so important. Job was fiercely attacked by Satan and yet did not sin (Job 1:22). That is to be our goal.

In fact, let's talk a little about that personal responsibility.

#6 { "I've never been exposed to satanic activities." }

Repeatedly we asked girls, "Have you ever been exposed to satanic activities?" Repeatedly they answered, "No." Then we asked them about specific things:

"HAVE YOU	ever looked at or read your horoscope?"
"HAVE YOU	ever participated in psychic activities?"
"HAVE YOU	ever had your palm read?"
"HAVE YOU	ever played a video game or watched a movie that portrayed demonic forces or witchcraft in a positive way?"

THE ANSWER CHANGED TO, "WELL, YEAH, BUT . . ." It's easy

to become comfortable with evil when we are exposed to it casually or repeatedly. And while casual exposure alone may not destroy your faith and values, you need to be aware that exposure plus a lack of awareness of what you're really exposed to can be dangerous. For example, if you think that a Ouija board is just a cute little game, you're missing the fact that it is considered to be a spiritual gateway to talk to the dead. (The Bible calls that "divination.") We're just saying: be *aware* of what you're getting close to and know what God says about it.

God forbids every form of witchcraft and sorcery, including things like fortune-telling, horoscopes, and communicating with the dead. God's Word spells this out in no uncertain terms:

Let no one be found among you . . . who practices divination or sorcery, interprets omens, engages in witchcraft, or casts spells, or who is a medium or spiritist or who consults the dead. Anyone who does these things is detestable to the LORD. (Deuteronomy 18:10–12 NIV)

I WILL SET MY FACE AGAINST
ANYONE WHO TURNS TO
MEDIUMS AND SPIRITISTS.
(LEVITICUS 20:6 NIV)

God's people are clearly to have nothing to do with divination, interpreting omens or signs (like horoscopes and fortune-telling), or anyone who is a medium or spiritist who consults the dead (like psychics). But psychic television shows are now mainstream, and even many Christians are being drawn into them. Seventy-two percent of youth-group attendees have read their horoscope.[6] We know of one group of girls that attempted to have a séance while they were at a Christian camp "just for fun."

We have to wonder if teens realize that these kinds of activities are not mere "innocent entertainment." God actually uses the word "detestable" to describe how He views such activities.

These warnings are not just found in the Old Testament. The apostle Paul clearly warns that those who practice sorcery or witchcraft will not inherit the kingdom of God (Galatians 5:20–21). If God is so intolerant of witchcraft, shouldn't we, at the very least, be cautious about exposing ourselves to it?

Witches, sorcerers, zombies, and other dead or occultic characters aren't considered something to fear, but are the stuff mainstream entertainment is made of. Often, we're looking for the "good" in them. Harry Potter? A "good" wizard. "Team Edward" because he's a "good" vampire. And recently in a theological conversation with some friends, a friend actually told one of us that *The Walking Dead* was the most positive spiritual programming on television.

Anything that presents characters of darkness as heroes, anything that incites curiosity or encourages experimentation and exploration of things related to the occult, is dangerous and should be avoided. To be entertained or enamored by witchcraft is to be lured into alliance with Satan himself, the declared archenemy of God. No wonder God despises witchcraft!

Here's another practice that you may not realize has occult connections.

Yoga is a popular exercise craze that is considered harmless, even beneficial, by many believers. But did you know that yoga is rooted in "the religious beliefs and practices of . . . Indian religions"?[7] Its original goal was achieving blissful union with the Supreme Brahman, the supreme spirit of Hinduism. The term *yoga* comes from the ancient Sanskrit word "yug," which

SATANIC ACTIVITIES & CHRISTIAN TEENS

So how many young women aged 13–19 actually have participated in things that are satanic? Researcher George Barna surveyed students who were actively involved in their youth groups and found that in the previous three months . . .

72% had looked at or read horoscopes

28% had had their palm read

42% had participated in psychic-related activities

82% had watched movies or other programming with paranormal or dark spiritual themes[8]

means "to yoke." Many of the positions of yoga were created to worship gods such as the sun and the moon.

YOU MIGHT BE SAYING, "WAIT A MINUTE! The yoga I practice

isn't tied to those occult practices. You can do it without worshiping. Just do the posturing and breathing and worship God instead." Well, then we'd ask, why not just do Pilates? It uses the same kind of breathing, similar posturing, and yields the same kinds of results physically but has no ties to pagan religions or idolatry.

Now, maybe you've read this whole chapter and you're thinking, *Whew! I'm glad I'm not involved in any activities that could be connected to occult practices.* Well, that doesn't necessarily mean that you're immune to Satan's influence. *Any* unholy practice or any unbiblical way of thinking can open you up to his activity in your life. Further, Scripture teaches that *attitudes* like anger (Ephesians 4:26–27), bitterness and unforgiveness (2 Corinthians 2:10–11), and rebellion against authority (1 Samuel 15:23) also make us vulnerable to Satan's influence.

WE WANT TO ENCOURAGE YOU TO EXAMINE YOUR LIFE. If you
are exposing yourself to any activities that could have occult connections, or if there is anger, unforgiveness, or rebellion in your heart, you are opening the door to the Enemy. Slam it shut!

Choose to forgive those who have wronged you. Make sure you renounce every evil practice you may have been engaged in or exposed to; then ask the Lord to forgive you and to release you from any foothold that Satan may have gained in your life through your choices. In this way, you will be cooperating with Christ who wants you to live in freedom.

The Bible says, "Stand fast therefore in the liberty by which Christ has made us free, and do not be entangled again with a yoke of bondage" (Galatians 5:1 NKJV). The "yoke of bondage" refers to the Old Testament law and religious rules. God doesn't want us to get caught up in trying to control our behavior with a bunch of external rules, but to be fully engaged in a love relationship with Jesus Christ—a relationship that motivates and enables us to walk in freedom and to live a life that is pleasing to Him.

The end of this verse gives us a word picture that helps us understand how we lose our freedom. The original Greek language, which ordered nouns and verbs quite differently from our English grammar, would have sounded more like this: "And not again in a yoke of slavery *entangle yourselves.*"[9] (Star Wars fans: you may think the Greeks talked a bit like Yoda!) For starters, this word makes pretty clear that we have some responsibility for our own enslavement, right? That's important to acknowledge.

But there's something else we want you to see here. The phrase "entangle yourselves" translates just one Greek word: *enechesthe.* This word means "to hold in or upon; to *ensnare.*" The Bible uses the concept of a snare quite often. It's a tool used to hunt and capture wild game. Now,

[lies young women believe]

maybe you're not a camo-loving hunter, but let's at least put a little orange vest on so we can venture into the woods to learn this lesson.

ENECHESTHE

Entangle yourselves, to hold in or upon; to ensnare

A snare isn't your typical steel foothold trap, which looks painful and nasty with its iron teeth. A snare is more subtle than that—a simple piece of cable that forms a loop. It appears nonthreatening, if it's even noticed at all. When an animal walks through a snare, it walks calmly. It just keeps walking, feeling nothing. Soon it may feel tension. But it presses forward. Before it even realizes it, the force of its own movement has enslaved it to the snare. It doesn't realize that if only it had backed out earlier, it could have gotten away. The animal is captured by the hunter, *but it is actually ensnared by its own actions!*

That's a picture of what can happen when we dabble in things of Satan, thinking them harmless. Ultimately, only Jesus can rescue us but we must be aware of how our own actions make us vulnerable, so we can repent and call out to Him when we feel the tightening of that snare around our hearts or minds!

If you make adjustments in your life in this area, you may find yourself standing alone. John 3:19 reminds us that, "People loved the darkness rather than the light." Many people don't want their lives exposed to God's Truth and light. They're afraid of what will be revealed. Don't be discouraged. Just keep inviting them to live in the light by showing them how much better it is than living in darkness.

DOUSING LIES WITH THE TRUTH

the lie

the truth

Everything bad that happens is spiritual warfare.

• Some of the bad things we face are battles with spiritual warfare. Ephesians 6:12

• Sometimes the bad things we face are brought on by our own choices. Romans 7:25; Galatians 5:16–18; 1 Peter 2:11

• Sometimes the bad things we face are brought on by the fallen world in which we live. John 15:18–19; 1 Corinthians 1:18–24; 1 John 2:15–17

• No matter the source, we are always responsible for our own choices and actions. Romans 14:10b, 12

I have never been exposed to satanic activities.

• God forbids every form of sorcery. Leviticus 20:6; Deuteronomy 18:10–12; Galatians 5:20–21

• Occult activities, along with sinful attitudes and choices, open the door to Satan's influence in our lives. Ephesians 4:26–27

[lies young women believe]

making it personal

IT'S DANGEROUS TO EXPOSE YOURSELVES TO LIES ABOUT SATAN, BUT WE DO IT EVERY DAY.

Examine your life by writing a journal entry that answers these questions:

What lies have I been most likely to believe about Satan?

What Scripture verses can I store in my heart to help me counter those lies with the Truth?

Bestie

I had SUCH a bummer day. Sometimes I just hate being a girl. Sometimes I find myself looking through magazines and comparing myself to people. I try to imitate the stars not because I admire them or their lives. #amIright? They just look perfect and I want to look perfect too. #sigh

Girl! You SO do not want to be a star. They are MESSED UP!! Check out Philippians 2:14–15. You are a STAR!!!!

THX! You always remind me to run to God's Word. #Truth

"The almost impossible thing, is to hand over your whole self—all your wishes and precautions—to Christ. . . . Until you have given up your self to Him you will not have a real self."

C. S. LEWIS

Lies about Myself

Paul Potts was a simple mobile phone salesman from South Wales. A rather rotund, middle-aged man with bad teeth, most people wouldn't have expected him to amount to much. Nor did he, for that matter. But his love for music and a bad stretch financially inspired him to put his own lack of confidence aside to sing for the world in hopes of winning $200,000. He decided to try out for a television contest called *Britain's Got Talent*, hosted by the curmudgeonly Simon Cowell and crew. This popular show is known to select the absolute best and the absolute worst to air. Which would Paul Potts be? It looked painfully apparent.

"Confidence has always been sort of a difficult thing for me," he said as he waited to go onstage.

"What are you here for today, Paul?" asked the beautiful female judge when he finally came out.

"To sing opera," he announced.

The judges rolled their eyes.

This was going to be good. Not only did he want to sing. He wanted to sing opera! Who would vote for that?

But moments later, the rich, lyric sounds of an Italian love song pouring out of this unknown singer released a flood of emotion in the audience and resulted in an outburst of cheers, tears, and a standing ovation. Paul Potts went on to sing his way into the number one spot on the show. Had he heeded his misgivings about himself, he'd never have realized that he was a world-class opera singer.

Our view of ourselves either enables us to do what God has created us to do or it limits us from becoming all He means for us to be. It is critical that you dismantle any lies you may believe about yourself. Let's look at two of the most common ones we found.

#7 { "Beautiful girls are worth more." }

As I (Nancy) was discussing this lie with a friend in her early twenties, she observed, "I don't think many girls would come out and say—or think—that they have to be as beautiful as an airbrushed model on a magazine, but we do have insanely unreal expectations for ourselves in this area." That's a fact!

Maybe you aren't going to make *People*'s 100 Most Beautiful list. Perhaps you don't look like the celebrities whose flawless faces and perfect bodies seem to be *everywhere*. We're sure hoping you don't make the same "fashion" decisions that many celebs make. Can we let you in on a little secret? Lean in. Listen closely. The women those magazines portray as the most beautiful, famous, and desirable women in the world struggle with the same lies we struggle with. Maybe even more so!

Just think about it: Hollywood is considered the "beauty capital" in the United States, yet where can you go to find more makeup artists, Botox salons, and plastic surgeons? Our beauty icons are paying a high price for fleeting fame and a fading spotlight. If true, lasting beauty doesn't come from a salon, where can we find it? In God's Word we find the assurance that we are already "fearfully and wonderfully made" (Psalm 139:14) and that the One whose opinion matters most finds us beautiful.

At the same time, we can certainly understand that the world's standard of so-called beauty can make it hard for you to see your own worth. Many of the girls we talked to said that they feel ugly or fat or both. Others said they hated themselves and felt worthless because of how they looked. There is an underlying sense that if you don't meet a certain standard of "beauty," you don't have value; you don't matter. Ouch! Lies we believe about our appearance can be deadly and so difficult to overcome. We can know the truth in our heads and still find ourselves reeling from the emotions of it all.

🍎 *I know that what is most important is who I am in Christ, but if I get emotional and quit thinking with my head, I start to feel like outer beauty is more important than inner beauty even though I know that's wrong. I abandon reason in favor of emotion.*

This year I even missed a lot of school because I was depressed about how I looked. I can get so worked up about my face or my hair or my

[lies young women believe]

body in the morning that it ruins my whole day. My mom has to drag me to school, and I run to the bathroom to check myself out one more time before I head to class. If I can't handle it, I call her and make up something about having cramps or whatever. I just hate that I get like this.

BEEN THERE? DONE THAT?

Though we've never gone quite that far, we have both battled with many of the same thoughts and emotions. When I (Nancy) was a young teen, I needed braces, was clueless about how to do anything with my hair, and had zero fashion sense. Further, I struggled with my weight throughout my teens. It was (and sometimes still is!) hard not to compare my short, chunky body with those tall, thin girls who could eat anything they wanted and who always looked terrific.

There's nothing new about our preoccupation with how things look on the outside. We're convinced it is something women have struggled with in every generation. In fact, it actually goes back to the first woman. Do you remember what appealed to Eve about the forbidden fruit?

**When the woman saw that the tree was good for food,
and that it was a delight to the eyes,
and that the tree was to be desired to make one wise,
she took of its fruit and ate.** (Genesis 3:6)

The fruit had function—it was good for food. It also appealed to Eve's desire for wisdom. But equally important, it was beautiful. The Enemy succeeded in getting her to value the physical appearance of a piece of fruit over less visible qualities such as trust and obedience. The problem wasn't that the fruit was beautiful, but that she placed physical appearance above her relationship with God. In doing so, she believed and acted on a lie. And we're still doing it today.

The list of how we act out is long:

SOME	check other girls out and enter into tremendous self-loathing.
SOME	check other girls out and say nasty things about them . . . or even in front of them.
SOME	will do just about anything to be affirmed by a guy. Anything!
SOME	cut themselves as punishment for not measuring up.
SOME	dress in such a way as to intentionally cause men to look and want.

SOME dress that way just to fit in, following the crowd's immodesty.

SOME flirt.

SOME overspend.

SOME just lie in bed and cry about it.

How do you stop the cycle?

First, remember that physical beauty is temporary. We realize that may not be what you wanted to hear! (Would it make you feel better if we reminded you that you're not alone in this?) You don't want a quick, temporary fix, do you? You want healing at the deepest level. So you've got to go to the Word of God for the Truth. It reminds us that "charm is deceitful, and beauty is vain" (Proverbs 31:30). Every older woman you know can attest to the fact that external beauty is fleeting and that our culture's obsession with staying young looking is an exercise in futility!

The average woman consumes 6 pounds of lipstick in her lifetime.
A SNAPPLE CAP

Thankfully, however, *there is a kind of beauty that does last*:

> **Do not let your adorning be external—**
> **the braiding of hair and the putting on of gold jewelry,**
> **or the clothing you wear—but let your adorning be the**
> **hidden person of the heart with the *imperishable beauty***
> **of a gentle and quiet spirit, which in God's sight**
> **is very precious.** (1 Peter 3:3–4)

These verses aren't saying you can't shop 'til you drop (as long as you don't overspend) or that having a great new haircut is sinful. Nowhere does Scripture condemn physical beauty or our expression of it. What is condemned is giving excessive attention to your outward beauty while you neglect the beauty of your heart!

I (Dannah) distinctly remember the turning point for me in my own struggle with beauty. I have always had problems with my skin. For most of my teen years, I so despised looking in the mirror that I learned to put my makeup on in the dark without a mirror. (My daughter Lexi still marvels at my blind mascara skills!) It was true that I did not have a clear complexion (I still don't!), but Satan used that fact to fuel lies. During those years, I often believed the lie that I was not just ugly, but that I had no value because of my skin.

In walked Jesus to the rescue! I was in college at Cedarville University when I finally realized that God didn't want just a quick-fix time of prayer with me every morning but that He wanted me to love Him with my whole heart and mind (Luke 10:27). I began to read the Word and pray more regularly. My journal turned from a gossip column to a recording of my prayers. And . . . sometime in the course of all that time with God . . . without ever realizing it . . . without ever praying about it . . . without ever focusing on it . . . I began to look in the mirror!

Now, I wasn't looking at it and saying, "Babe, you are hot!" But I was also not fearfully avoiding it. No, I was looking in the mirror and simply sensing, "God made a good thing." You will likely never be at peace with how God created you until you grasp this: you've got to be more focused on your internal beauty than your external looks!

Recently, a friend who had just seen a video of me (Nancy) that was made a couple decades ago tactfully tried to point out how much I've aged since then. (It didn't help that I used to color my prematurely gray hair in those days—I've since thrown away the bottle and just go *au naturale*!) We had a good laugh about it. Then I said to my friend, "You know, I'm really OK with this aging stuff. I decided long ago that I was not going to spend my life trying to stay young looking or obsessed with physical beauty!"

That's true. However, I've also determined that I *will* spend my life trying to cultivate inner beauty—becoming more loving, gracious, and kind. I've seen women of every age who wouldn't be characterized as physical knockouts, but who radiate an inner beauty that is truly captivating and that can only be attributed to their relationship with Jesus.

Here's a simple test to determine if you're focused on the kind of beauty that lasts:

TODAY DID YOU SPEND MORE TIME:

in front of the mirror, making yourself beautiful
on the outside **or in God's Word,**
developing inner beauty of heart and character?

It's that simple. God wants you to groom your heart. **The beauty that matters most to God is on the inside, but it will be reflected in how you present yourself on the outside.** Your sense of fashion should reflect what's inside. The apostle Paul wrote about how women should dress. He encouraged women to "adorn themselves in respectable apparel, with modesty and self-control, not with braided hair and gold or pearls or costly attire, but with what is proper for women who profess godliness" (1 Timothy 2:9–10).

Your outward appearance should reflect your heart. Your heart should be pure. That's why modesty is so important. Your heart should be joyful. That's why we give a big thumbs-down to the dark goth style. Your heart should be filled with life. That's why the trendy skull and crossbones should be passed up. What is on the outside should be a representation of what's on the inside.

What you believe about beauty will be determined by where you look. We admit that it's hard to separate the inside and the outside. That's why we're going to go right to the heart of another really important issue: *comparing ourselves.* Many of the Christian girls we talked to had stacks of beauty magazines at home. And perusing them didn't seem to be doing anything good. Here's what a few said:

 A lot of advertisers are saying, "We are starting to use real models, ones that aren't so skinny." But the real models are still skinnier than the majority of people. It makes me feel like I'm not that skinny and that I'm never going to get anywhere.

 I get this kind of high while I'm looking at fashion websites. I kind of think that I'll look like that, but then I look in the mirror and I find myself worse off than before. I'll never look like that.

Would it help you to be reminded that even the women on those fashion websites don't look like that? Kate Winslet is a British actress and singer who has won an Academy Award, an Emmy Award, four Golden Globe Awards, a Grammy Award, and more. When she was featured on the cover of a popular magazine looking svelte and sexy, she responded:

 "I do not look like that and more importantly, I don't desire to look like that. . . . They've reduced the size of my legs by about a third."[1]

These high-paid, glamorous women just don't look the same way we see them on magazine covers and in movies. And they feel the same pressure you feel to measure up to an unhealthy, unattainable standard, as another well-known actress acknowledged:

 "I'm twice the size, height and everything else of most of the other actresses who are going for an audition. It's mad, isn't it? When you realize that even at my size I'm one of the largest there. It's at the point you start to say, 'I don't think it'd be healthy for me to stay here much longer.'"[2]

The press estimates her height at 5'7" and her weight to be about 115 pounds. She probably wears a size 2 or 4 most of the time. And she's big??!

The world's standard of outward beauty is unattainable.

God's standard of beauty can be achieved by time spent alone with Him, and that inner beauty will make you confident with what God has given you on the outside.

#8 { "I have to perform to be loved and accepted." }

A whopping 95 percent of the girls we spoke to admitted that they are always or sometimes plagued by this lie.

🍎 *I have been struggling with depression for five years. I always have those little feelings that I'm not worth anything—that I'm not good enough. I can tell it is Satan telling me that I am never going to make it. That I can't DO anything in my life.*

🍎 *As soon as you get into high school, everything you do becomes about college. If you make a bad grade, everyone points it out. Every day you feel this tremendous pressure that the decisions you are making will affect your ability to get into college. It's always in the back of your mind.*

🍎 *I want to get a scholarship to play ball in college. If I have a bad game, Satan will tell me, "You did bad in this game . . . and on top of that these things are wrong with you. . . ." I feel like that is how everyone sees me.*

Are you sure that is how everyone sees you? It might *feel* like everyone, including God and your parents, is judging you based on your performance. But is that true? Let's begin to expose this lie by first looking at God's view of you.

Your value is not determined by what you do, but by how God views you. I (Dannah) loved each of my children before I even met them. There's Robby, my wonder boy and firstborn. There's Lexi, my artistic beauty born just three years later. And then there's Autumn, my

whimsical and brave adopted daughter from China. I dreamed of them and thought of them and prayed for them before they were even conceived or adopted. I could barely wait to hold them when they arrived. And, I'm human! How much more does God love *you*—His child?

He chose you before the world was created (Ephesians 1:4). He knit you together in your mother's womb and declared that you have been "wonderfully made" (Psalm 139:14). He loved you before you could love Him (1 John 4:9). And, if you belong to Him, nothing can ever separate you from His love (Romans 8:38–39). Your value isn't determined by what you do. It's determined by the simple fact that you are.

God doesn't need you to do important things; He just wants you to be obedient. A prominent magazine for business leaders has referred to your generation as a "rising superpower."[3] That description came from two stand-out characteristics found in a study of college freshmen:[4] a strong drive to succeed, and more students than ever considering themselves to be gifted. Those two qualities sometimes lead people to conclude that your generation is self-absorbed. However, there's another quality that we think is encouraging. When measuring benevolent behavior, recent college freshmen have proven to be strongly interested in activism, and are more likely than those before to volunteer their services and to give money to charities.[5]

PENNING YOUR **PERFORMANCE** FEARS

Your parents aren't God, so it is possible that they could be obsessed with your performance at school or in sports or another area where you excel. However, it's a lot more likely that you just *perceive* that they are obsessed with your performance. How can you know? Talk to them! If you find it hard to express your feelings face-to-face, try writing them a letter. We've seen relationships powerfully healed through letters. A letter gives you the chance to say what you feel and to change anything that might be too negative or disrespectful. Why not try one and see what God does with it?

Along with these characteristics and behaviors is a growing sense that you need to make a mark on the world by the time you're a legal adult, to really count at all. An appearance on *Shark Tank* or a groundbreaking Etsy store before you're in high school. A viral social media post that makes you famous in two minutes (literally) or a publishing contract by age eighteen.

It doesn't matter how, but today's "rising superpowers" are expected to accomplish great things in great ways.

Translate all that "rising superpower" stuff to the Christian community, and you may have become convinced that you have a "life calling" to "do something great for God." *This can be a dangerous way of thinking.* It might surprise you to read that, but there's a difference between having a calling to do something great "for God" and being called to serve a great God. The subtle difference between these two is critical. Having a calling to do something great for God puts the focus (and burden) on you and how great you are. Having a calling to serve a great God keeps the focus on Him and frees you to just obey Him. Are you sincerely looking for a calling from God, or truth be told, are you really looking to be famous?

And consider this: fame in the Christian world doesn't come the way you might think.

> **Mary, the mother of our Lord,** became "famous" by simply saying "yes, Lord" to a life that promised she would be an outcast in her own community, give birth in a barn, and live in hiding in a foreign country.

> **Corrie ten Boom** became "famous" by simply saying "yes, Lord," when that meant hiding Jews during the Holocaust and spending years in a Nazi concentration camp living with fleas and eating stone-cold porridge when she had any food at all.

> **Elisabeth Elliot** became "famous" by simply saying "yes, Lord" when her husband was martyred at the hand of Huaorani warriors in Ecuador and then again when God asked her to return and love those people in spite of what they'd done.

> **Amy Carmichael,** one of the first evangelical human trafficking opponents, became "famous" by saying "yes, Lord" to serving in India for fifty-five years without a furlough and by being bedridden with illness for two decades while she rescued unloved children and sex workers.

These women had no microphones, no podcasts, no blog, and no stages. They had one thing: obedience. God doesn't need you to do something great. He wants you to be obedient moment by moment. And as you do, He will use you as He sees fit.

The notion that you can do something to have value or to earn God's love is heretical. At the root of this lie is a mindset that is based on *works* rather than *grace* (Romans 11:6). Responding to God's love, which He expressed profoundly in the death of His precious Son, is all that is required for you to experience His favor. Rather than trying to *do* something for Him (works-based), you need to receive what *He* has done for you (grace-based)! You can't get this free gift through works because then you could boast that you earned it (Ephesians 2:9). Christ died so that you can experience God's love and acceptance as a gift of grace.

YOUR GOOD WORKS ARE TO GLORIFY GOD, NOT YOURSELF

Whether you're a swimmer, a ball player, a straight-A student, or the leader of your youth group, every effort you put forth should be for God's glory, not your own (1 Corinthians 10:31). If you are feeling pressure for the things that you *do* to make you valuable, you are doing them for the wrong reasons. God does want you to do good things, but only as an offering back to Him for His great gift to us (James 2:12–18).

Sophia found that she was in a destructive pattern of believing that her performance gave her value. From an early age, she competed as a swimmer at the international level.

 When I was eleven, my mother moved us three hundred miles so that I could swim. This ingrained in my mind that swimming was what mattered. It was where I could prove my value.

When she was sixteen, she became a follower of Christ. In spite of a budding faith, she began to believe the lie that her identity was swimming, and to please God, she had to do well at swimming.

 I looked up to Christian athletes. In order to be that, I had to be a good athlete, and that meant being the best at swimming.

She was soon invited to swim on scholarship at a Big Ten university, competing at a higher level than ever before. But she was miserable.

 It took me three to four years after I surrendered my life to Christ, to figure out that my identity was found in Christ and that my grades and swimming were not what gave me value.

It's OK if you are an athlete who is called of God and is proud of accomplishments, but it is not good for those accomplishments to be your identity. I had to quit. Stopping was the hardest thing up to that point in my life. It felt awful! My identity collapsed at first. I had

a time of mourning and I isolated myself from people. I went through depression. I even hacked my hair off. But eventually, I began to know that I was valuable just because I was God's girl. It was worth the pain to find this Truth.

Swimming wasn't bad in and of itself. But it had become Sophia's measure of her own worth—her "works," which she thought gave her value in the eyes of her mom, her peers, and even her God.

Often the things we find value in are good things. This has been a recurring battle for me (Nancy). As a teen, I was tempted to find my identity—my sense of worth—in academic achievement or in my abilities as a classical pianist. Now, as an older woman, I sometimes measure my value by my "performance" as a speaker or an author.

When I hit a "home run," I feel affirmed and secure; when I do "so-so," I easily become discouraged and vulnerable to self-doubt. I have to consciously counter those feelings with the Truth that I am fully accepted *in Christ* and that my worth to Him (or others) has nothing to do with my performance. Otherwise, I tend to drive myself endlessly and to always be looking for positive feedback on "how I'm doing."

That kind of thinking is prideful, performance-based Christianity. Actually, it is diametrically opposed to true Christianity, which from start to finish is based on humble faith in *Christ's* performance and the underserved, unmerited grace of God!

If you have a tendency to define your value by your performance, you may need to take some time off from one or more things you do to find value, in order to rest in the free grace of God. But you don't want to just drop everything and show disrespect for team members, teachers, and church coworkers. **Move cautiously.**

First of all, talk to your parents. Tell them how much pressure you feel. It's likely that just talking with them will help alleviate the pressure. Ask God to give your parents wisdom as they counsel and advise you.

Second, listen to the advice of your parents and your church leaders. Ask them if there is anything you need to step back from for a season or permanently in order to learn to rest in your value as a child of God.

Wrestle with this one now, because it won't go away. It'll just grow with you. And the bigger it gets, the heavier a weight it becomes in your life. Choose now to embrace the Truth that as a believer in Christ, you have value—not because of anything you do, but simply because you are God's girl, redeemed and loved by the grace of God, because of what Christ has done for you!

the lie

the truth

Beautiful girls are worth more.

• Physical beauty is only temporary. Proverbs 31:30; 1 Peter 3:3–5

• The beauty that matters most to God is on the inside. 1 Timothy 2:9–10

• What you believe about beauty is determined by where you look. 1 Peter 3:3–4

I have to perform to be loved and accepted.

• Your value is not determined by what you do, but by how God views you. Ephesians 1:4; Psalm 139:14; 1 John 4:9; Romans 8:38–39

• The notion that you can do something to earn love and have value is heretical. Ephesians 2:9; Romans 11:6

• Your good works are to glorify God, not yourself. 1 Corinthians 10:31; James 2:12–18

making it personal

Often at the root of our most deeply embedded sinful habits are lies we believe about ourselves. If only we could believe who God says we are! Grab your journal again. It's time to get some Truth into your heart. Consider these questions as you write:

What lies have I been most likely to believe about myself?

What Scripture verses can I store in my heart to help me counter those lies with the Truth?

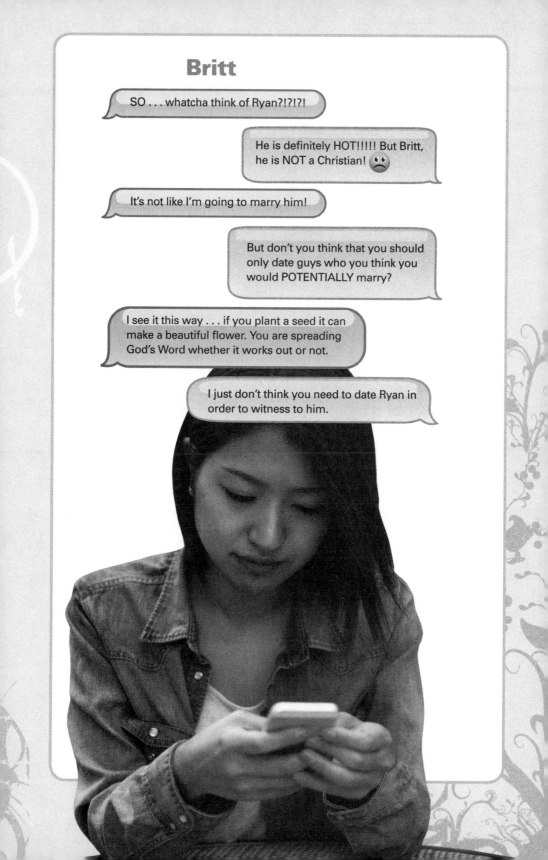

"It is a safe thing to trust
Him to fulfill the desires
which He creates."

AMY CARMICHAEL (1867–1951),
MISSIONARY TO INDIA

Lies about Sexuality

WARNING: **You've just entered the most controversial and heart-wrenching chapter in this book.** We want to invite you to stop right now and pray. Yes, we really mean it. We believe that the lies girls believe about guys, sexuality, and sex are some of the most powerful lies and have the potential to expose girls' hearts to deep, long-term hurt.

God's Word explains that the marriage relationship between a man and a woman is an earthly picture of Christ and His love for us. That theme is woven throughout both the Old and New Testaments. One of the main reasons why God designed marriage was to give us a picture of His passion and His sacrificial love for His people. And that's one reason why He wants marriages to be pure. When the marriage or sexual relationship is defiled, that defiles the sacred picture of God's love. If your future marriage has the potential to show the world the incredible love and grace of God, doesn't it make sense that Satan would want to try to destroy that picture?

Stop right now and ask God to open your eyes and your heart to the Truth as you read through this chapter.

OK, let's go.

#9 { "It's OK to date whoever I feel like dating." }

For the most part, the girls we've spoken to agree that they should not *marry* a non-Christian. At the same time, many of them don't feel as strongly about *dating* non-Christians:

I really want to marry a Christian, but I'm not looking for marriage right now, so [implied] it's OK to date guys who don't follow Jesus.

I don't really think it matters if the guys I date are Christians or not. For one, we're just in high school. I don't think religion is a big issue right now.

 Sometimes it's fun to just go out and have fun and flirt and all that stuff and not take everything so seriously.

We're not going to go easy on you here. This is a huge issue with more serious, potential implications for your own personal life and the kingdom of Christ than you may realize.

From start to finish, the Bible tells the story of marriage between one man and one woman being a picture of Christ's love for His bride, the church. Ephesians 5:31–32 makes this clear:

> "A MAN SHALL LEAVE HIS FATHER AND MOTHER AND HOLD FAST TO HIS WIFE, AND THE TWO WILL BECOME ONE FLESH." THIS MYSTERY IS PROFOUND, BUT I AM SAYING IT REFERS TO CHRIST AND THE CHURCH.

Marriage is a picture of a beautiful, powerful spiritual Truth. So can you understand why Satan would want to lie to you about its value and meaning and would want to set you up to tarnish this amazing picture? If you want to preserve God's purpose and intent for marriage—and if you want to experience His greatest blessings in your life, you can't afford to just date anyone you *feel* like dating. You must determine not to date anyone who doesn't know and love Jesus and who is not fully committed to following Him.

God's Word is clear that we should not form binding relationships with unbelievers (2 Corinthians 6:14–18). Marriage is the ultimate binding relationship. God does not want you to be tied to an unbeliever in marriage—and the power to live out that conviction begins now. If you compromise now, you'll be far more likely to compromise when you're ready for marriage.

Don't tell yourself, "It's just a casual relationship. I would never marry this guy." Maybe not. But if you invest time, interest, effort, and thought into a relationship that is unwise . . . sooner or later, your feelings will grow stronger. And once your emotions are involved, you may well find yourself making life-impacting decisions you never dreamed you would make. Because even though our feelings are not facts, they sure are powerful.

This is one area where there is no room for compromise. Satan is seeking to rob you of a future filled with joy, peace, and the opportunity to glorify God with your life. It's just not worth trading all that in for a relationship with someone who doesn't have a heart for God and for a future that could end up filled with pain and heartache.

Over the years, many women have poured out their hearts to us about deep regrets they have over choices they made related to dating, courtship, and marriage. They would give anything to be able to go back and relive that part of their lives. Unfortunately, that's just not possible. As I (Nancy) listen to these women share their heartaches, I often think, "I wish every young woman could hear this story—before it's too late!"

Now, while we're talking about dating . . . since this book was originally published, we've seen this trend to follow your feelings grow to include not just dating *guys* who aren't Christians, but *girls*, too. One of our readers recently wrote to say:

 I'm thirteen and a Christian. I have believed that I might be bisexual for a long time and I'm dating a girl . . . just for now, not for forever or marriage or anything.

Today's gender revolution screams, "Do whatever you *feel* is right for you." The freedom to experiment with bisexuality and lesbianism is not only considered OK, but is viewed as compassionate and affirming to those struggling with gender confusion or same-sex attraction. To help us understand why our feelings can't govern our dating relationships, let's go back to the basics. The design of sex begins with the meaning of male and female. The opening chapter of God's Word makes that clear:

>>
Then God said, "Let us make man in our image, after our likeness. . . .

So God created man in his own image, in the image of God he created him; male and female he created them. (Genesis 1:26–27)

God created mankind in His image. And He created two distinct biological sexes—male and female—to reflect something about Himself. What did He want to reflect? Well, this side of heaven we may never fully understand why He created two biological sexes, but we can begin with the realization that God is a relational being. This relationship is clearly seen in the Trinity.

God the Father, God the Son, and God the Holy Spirit are distinct persons and yet they are one God, one in essence. One man and one woman—also distinctly different—when joined together in marriage display a similar oneness, too.

What happens the moment the first man and woman meet one another on the pages of Genesis? They are married. Right there in the Garden of Eden. Genesis tells us:

> THEREFORE A MAN SHALL LEAVE HIS FATHER
> AND HIS MOTHER AND HOLD FAST TO HIS WIFE,
> AND THEY SHALL BECOME ONE FLESH. (2:24)

The male and female are two distinct, independent humans but when they come together in the covenant of marriage they become one.

God's intention in marriage is to display the beautiful unity of God the Father, God the Son, and God the Holy Spirit as One.

That's all very well and good, but even someone who knows all this can be tempted by intense desires for a relationship that isn't healthy or wise, or that doesn't reflect the union of God. So here's what we've got to keep in mind: *feelings aren't facts.* Our feelings can fluctuate wildly, and are often tied to changing circumstances rather than reality. In fact, the Bible reveals that the heart—including our feelings—apart from the grace and indwelling Spirit of God, is deceitful and wicked (Jeremiah 17:9).

FEELINGS aren't FACTS

The most important thing about your sexuality is not how you feel but what God says is true. (That wouldn't be a bad sentence to repeat to yourself every day!)

You are a female image bearer of God. And your sexuality and future marriage (if that's God's plan for you) are intended to help you carry God's image and His redeeming love to our sinful, broken world. And, following His plan will always prove to be the safest, healthiest, and most satisfying choice for your heart in the long run.

We want to spare you the kind of heartache so many women—younger and older—have experienced. We want you to enjoy God's very best for the rest of your life. So we're going to give you a challenge. We want to urge you to make a serious commitment. (You may think you're too young to even be thinking about dating, much less marriage! But *now* is the time to develop wise, godly convictions.) Here's the challenge:

You may think that standard sounds unnecessarily high for "casual dating." But think about it—if you never date someone who would not be qualified to be a godly husband, you will significantly decrease your chances of dishonoring the Lord or ending up in long-term heartache. We're confident this is one commitment you'll never regret making!

#10 { "I need a boyfriend." }

One day I (Nancy) was discussing this book with a young friend who loves the Lord and is actively involved in ministry. When we got to the topic of guys, she immediately resonated with this lie. *"Yes!"* she said. "The drive for male attention is a *huge* issue for us! We are so programmed to believe that we're not valuable until we have attention and acceptance from guys!"

More than two-thirds of our focus group respondents admitted that they "feel better about their lives when they have a boyfriend." This lie was equally pervasive among all school types—public, Christian, and homeschooled. Nor did there seem to be any correlation to whether a girl had ever had a boyfriend. Bottom line: a lot of you feel the need for a guy in your life.

 It's not like I really have to have a boyfriend, but I do like the confirmation that someone likes me.

 At school it is really hard as a Christian to try to stand up for waiting for the right guy to come along. It is really pushed to have a boyfriend, because that is what everyone else does.

 I would feel so much better right now if I had a boyfriend.

After seeing these results, I (Dannah) was so deeply troubled that I sought to try to better define the problem and provide a solution. My research led me back to Genesis to discover what I have come to call "the Craving."

The Craving is a part of the curse. It dates all the way back to Eve and that first lie . . . and sin . . . in the Garden of Eden. After she and Adam sinned, God showed up to explain that things would never be the same. He described to them the new conditions of living since sin had entered the world. To Eve, he said:

BOY CRAZY QUOTIENT

We asked young women to respond to the statement "I would feel better about my life if I had a boyfriend."

68% Always or sometimes agree

32% Never agree

> YOUR DESIRE SHALL BE FOR YOUR HUSBAND, AND HE SHALL RULE OVER YOU.
>
> (GENESIS 3:16 NKJV)

The word **DESIRE** is critical here. It's also controversial. Some theologians say it means Eve would have an obsessive desire for her husband. Others say it means she would have a desire to control her husband. For sure, sin has impacted us negatively in both ways: both in a desire to resist a husband's leadership, and in an unhealthy desire or obsession for a man. It's fair to say that, as a result of sin, Eve's once pure, healthy relationship with her husband would become twisted and unhealthy.

Actually, the two interpretations may not be all that far apart. It's clear that many women spend much of their young lives (and probably some of their older years) obsessing about getting a guy! The original Hebrew word for desire in Genesis 3:16 comes from a root word that means "to stretch out after; or to run after."[1] As I watch young women struggle with the Craving to have a guy, I think they also often have a deep desire to be in control. That is to say, the desire to have a guy grows into the desire to control a guy!

Here's how I've seen girls live out the progression:

A woman I met at a Christian college this month asked me this question, "My boyfriend hasn't told me he loves me yet. Is it OK for me to go first?"

[lies young women believe]

One girl I mentored for a while told me it was old-fashioned to wait for a guy to ask her out, so she intended to do the asking.

Another girl I mentored had really good intentions in always leading her boyfriend to study the Bible with her. She was always the one who asked if they could pray at the end of a date. But her question to me was this: "Why doesn't he ever ask if we can read the Bible? Why doesn't he ask if we can pray?" She couldn't see that she wasn't making room for him to lead.

On the surface it may look like these women have strong, "normal" cravings to *have* a guy. But when you take a closer look, under that longing is the craving to be in control of and lead the relationship. If you intend to one day live within a marriage where the husband lovingly and sacrificially leads the wife, as God's Word instructs, then you have to begin now to be content and to let the guy do the leading!

The Craving is dangerous. It may begin as a middle-school infatuation with guys, but it grows into something bigger that seeks to be in control of and overwhelm your life. The answer isn't to deny your desire, but to understand and redirect it.

Over the years, I've thought a lot about a verse in Proverbs that I think speaks to this:

WHAT IS DESIRED IN A MAN IS STEADFAST LOVE, AND A POOR MAN IS BETTER THAN A LIAR. (19:22)

This verse acknowledges that people desire true (steadfast, unfailing) love. And this desire is not something we should be afraid to admit. It's better to be poor in love than to deny the need. But guess what? The love you're looking for doesn't come from a guy. There's only one source for unfailing love: God.

If marriage is a picture of our relationship with Christ, you must know the love of Christ to paint it. Stretch out after and run hard to the love of God, not guys.

Here's why I prefer to call this strong desire for a guy "the Craving" rather than boy craziness. Boy craziness is considered unharmful and "normal." (It's also "normal" to lie, experience sibling rivalry, or disobey. But each of those "normal" things can be recognized as both harmful and sinful.) In reframing the language of how we crave guys, I hope to help you see that it can be both harmful and even sinful. I mean, when we place a guy on a pedestal of longing that belongs to God and His love, we've created an idol for our hearts, right?

No guy ever has been the source of unfailing love! So stop trying to be in control of getting and keeping a guy. Instead, spend your energy running after the real source of satisfaction. If you first pursue a love relationship with Jesus, not only will He satisfy the deepest craving of your heart, but someday God may be pleased to give you a husband who will be a picture to you of His powerful, unfailing love.

Remember, God did not design marriage first and foremost, but He designed a love relationship between us and Him that is portrayed in marriage. You can't paint a picture of something you haven't seen. Spend your time pursuing a love relationship with God and allow Him to be in control of whether or not He intends for you to paint a picture of it through marriage.

When you look to a relationship with a guy to satisfy your deepest longings, you're setting yourself up for a lifetime of disappointment, and potentially for disaster. That's what happened to Samantha. She was a strong believer—a leader in her community and church—when she fell for the lie that she had to have a boyfriend.

I never intended to end up here. I just wanted a boyfriend. The one I got seemed amazing to me. He said he wanted to be pure and wanted to be involved in church with me. Early on I noticed that he struggled with some things that freaked me out—like drugs, but I was pretty certain I could help him overcome them. I just wasn't willing to let anything get in the way of having my boyfriend. Pretty soon I was pulled in too.

The next thing I knew, it was my senior year of high school and I was pregnant. I guess that's when I started to believe that it would all be OK if we just got married. We loved God. So we got married the week I graduated, with my belly nice and round. Well, that worked for about two years. Then he left. So now I'm nineteen and I have this amazing toddler and I love her, but life is just . . . well, hard. I wish I could go back to my fifteen-year-old self and tell myself, "You don't have to have a guy." There was no lasting happiness in it.

The Song of Solomon is the most romantic book of the Bible. It describes a love relationship between King Solomon and his bride. Three times in this passionate love story, the young woman expresses a commitment not to "stir up" or "awaken" love until it pleases (2:7; 3:5; 8:4). What in the world does that mean?

The MacArthur Study Bible explains what it means when Solomon's bride purposes not to "awaken love until it pleases":

> [She] knows that the intensity of her love for Solomon cannot yet be experienced until the wedding, so she invites [her friends] to keep her accountable regarding sexual purity. Up to this point, the escalating desire of the Shulamite for Solomon has been expressed in veiled and delicate ways as compared to the explicit and open expressions which follow, as would be totally appropriate for a married couple.[2]

This bride-to-be has intense love and desires for the man she is going to marry. There is nothing wrong with those desires—they are God-created! But she knows those desires can only be appropriately expressed or fulfilled *after* she and this man are united in covenant marriage. So she determines not to awaken those desires—not to fuel them until the time when they can legitimately be fulfilled.

GOD DOES NOT WANT YOU TO "AWAKEN LOVE" UNTIL THE TIME IS RIGHT.

God has good reasons for instructing us not to awaken love prematurely. Being in relationships with guys early often leads to sexual sin. Research tells us that girls who have boyfriends by seventh grade are among those most likely to be sexually active in their high school years. Further, being in a relationship with a guy six months or longer is one of the top five factors that leads to early sexual activity in teenagers.[3] As your heart becomes entwined in a relationship, you'll have a hard time sticking to your standards of purity.

So when is the time right to awaken love? It's appropriate to start "stirring up" love when you're at a place in life that you're ready to begin thinking about getting married and when God has brought a man into your life who is ready to commit himself to you as your husband for a lifetime. Your parents and other godly friends and leaders in your life will be able to help you confirm that "this is the guy."

After you walk down the aisle and say "I do" to the man God has chosen to be your husband, *then* it's time to let love be *fully awakened* and to enjoy it with unrestrained freedom and passion—for the glory of God!

It saddens us to see teen girls wasting time by taking on the kinds of attachments and responsibilities that come with marriage—in tenth grade!— when instead they could be fostering their relationship with Christ. Mia took a drastic step to change that. She decided to start using the time she had spent pursuing guys getting to know God instead:

I was completely boy crazy in tenth grade. My parents were worried. I wasn't dating guys, per se. But I felt this unquenchable desire to have a boyfriend. My mom helped me plan something really cool. For one year of my life—my junior year—I was going to concentrate completely on my relationship with God. In addition to my daily devos, I spent one weekend evening a week just "with" Him. My heart was just focused on Him. After about two months, I was like, "Guys? What guys?" It was one of the best years of my high school career.

#11 { "It's not really sex." }

We're really into purity—my boyfriend and I. So, we try to speak about it at events and stuff. We tell people that they can just do what we do. Just have oral sex.

He was just a friend, but before I knew it, we were sending these trashy Snaps back and forth. We became sort of electronic friends with benefits, but we never had real sex.

[lies young women believe]

🍎 *Honestly, there's not one guy in my youth group who I haven't kissed or touched in some way. Some of them got farther than others, but I have a line I won't cross. I've never had sex.*

WHOA! Those comments may express the way most girls think. But

they don't reflect the way God thinks. And nothing less than His way of thinking will bring you joy and satisfaction in the long run. Ephesians 5:3 (NIV) defines God's standard of purity: "But among you there must not be *even a hint* of sexual immorality." This certainly includes actually having sex. But the sexual sin forbidden here is broader than that. There should not be even a hint of sex outside of the marriage bed. You don't have to have physical contact with a guy to "hint" at sexual sin. Jesus extended the definition of sexual sin to include looking at someone and lusting after them (Matthew 5:28).

YOU "HINT"	at sex when you wear a low-cut tank top showing off your cleavage.
YOU "HINT"	at sex when you post a mildly pornographic photo as your profile pic.
YOU "HINT"	at sex when you send a trashy text message to someone.
YOU "HINT"	at sex when you look at mild online porn.
YOU "HINT"	at sex when you expose yourself to songs, television shows, and movies that use sexual humor and language. (The very next verse says, "Let there be no filthiness nor foolish talk nor crude joking, which are out of place"— Ephesians 5:4.)

According to Jesus, these areas of mental and visual impurity count. They rob you of virtue. And often of your reputation.

Recently, I (Dannah) was called in to a Christian high school to meet with an entire class of middle school girls who got caught up in sexting. They'd been sending *each other* nearly naked and a few fully naked snaps of themselves as jokes. Shower photos. Bathroom photos. Locker room selfies. They weren't overtly sexual photos, just super silly "girls being girls." That's what they told the police officer who showed up at their school to tell them they had been hacked by a sexual predator. Here's where it gets really complicated. Technically, many of the photos were child porn

IS IT **JUST** FASHION?

Miniskirts. Low-plunging camis. Skin-tight T's. You may be tempted to believe that dressing in some of today's common fashion trends is OK. But is it?

Girls, if we love God, we will want to please Him in every area of our lives—including what we wear. His Word makes clear that He wants us to be respectable and modest in how we dress and act (1 Timothy 2:9).

Recently, my (Nancy's) husband and I were talking about how sad it makes us to see suggestive, revealing photos of beautiful young women we know and love, posted on social media. We're guessing these girls think they just look fashionable and cute. But we wondered aloud if they have any idea of the message they're sending (much like the foolish woman in Proverbs 7:10), and how bombarded their Christian brothers feel by clothing and photos that emphasize the sexual allure of women.

The work it takes for these guys to keep their minds pure can be exhausting. We don't want to make it harder on them (Romans 14:13)!

We're also called to save the deepest treasures of our beauty for just one man (Proverbs 5:18–19), not to share them with every guy that walks by. Let's keep all this in mind when we decide how to dress and what photos to take and share with others.

and the state didn't have any age restrictions on who could be charged. So, the only way the state could legally deal with the girls was to categorize them as child porn traffickers, which they had to do in order to bring the predator to justice. Ouch!

God doesn't want you to get caught up in sexting—whether it's silly photos to girlfriends or sexual photos to romantic interests— because He wants to keep your body, your mind, your heart, and your reputation safe.

But sexual sin of the mind and eyes isn't the only area where Christian young women are struggling. Our hearts break as we hear of young women engaged in practices ranging from sexual touching to compulsive masturbation to oral sex, all the while rationalizing that these acts are not sexual sin.

They are.

God's standard of purity is high, but the rewards are worth the price of self-control. The world will try to tell you that you are missing out. That's not really true. You see, God knows we're prone to question the value and necessity of His rules. We wonder, *What in the world is the purpose of this one? How can it be good?* (Much as Eve questioned God's limitations about the Tree of the Knowledge of Good and Evil.) The answer is that all His rules exist so we will prosper (Deuteronomy 6:24). Following that line of reasoning, God's limitations on sexuality are given, in part, to make the gift more fantastic. But is that really true?

Social science says it is. In one of the most liberal studies conducted on the sex lives of Americans,[4] it was discovered that those who did not engage in sex prior to marriage were more sexually satisfied. It went on to further state that the "religiously active" were among the most sexually satisfied. God is not withholding something from you. He wants you to wait—so you can experience the greatest possible sexual fulfillment—in a covenant marriage relationship, if marriage is His will for your life one day.

We have met lots of women who earnestly wish they had been willing to wait for God's timing for physical intimacy. In many cases, they have paid painful consequences for not doing so. We've also known some who made the tough choice to wait.

Stephanie Canfield is enjoying the benefits of that choice today:

When I was in junior high I made a commitment to God, my parents, and myself to stay sexually pure until marriage. I made a list of character qualities I wanted in my husband. As time went on, I thought I must have set my expectations too high. I didn't know any guys who had the same standards I did. Some of my friends told me this guy didn't exist!

During my senior year of high school, I almost gave up on my dream to find him. I started to believe it could never happen, so I rushed ahead of God and caved into the pressure to begin a relationship (against my parents' advice). I soon experienced consequences—in my relationship with God, my friends, and my parents. God convicted me, and I surrendered my future to Him once again.

Eventually, God had someone saved for me, and in His perfect timing He brought him along. I discovered that the way of purity is far better, even though it requires patience and a willingness to go against the flow. The outcome is worth every sacrifice and makes marriage all the sweeter.

Stephanie's husband, Jeremiah, agrees:

 I told God when I was younger that I would lock all my emotions and desires to win a lady's heart in a box and that I would give Him the key.

I said I wanted Him to open this box in my heart when the right one came along. It was such a joy and thrill to give everything to Stephanie. I don't regret for one moment not "dating around." I had no past relationship scars to tell my wife about; I was saving myself for her alone.

I now get to spend the rest of my life pouring out my love on a woman who has my whole heart and affection.

Wouldn't you love for a man to say that kind of thing about you someday? When you wait for the right guy and you both follow His plan for your relationship, you'll have the joy of God's blessing on your marriage!

#12 { "I can't handle the loneliness of staying pure." }

One of the saddest moments in the focus groups was when a young girl enrolled in a *Christian middle school* gave voice to the great loneliness many of you feel in your quest for purity. She said:

 I think that at my school, having sex is normal. Everybody has either had sex or they are really close to it. That is something I struggle with a lot. I wonder if I am going to wait. It is all about the moment for me. I struggle with waiting.

SHE WASN'T ALONE among teens we interacted with. While the vast majority of respondents disagreed with the statement "I feel like I am the only person not having sex," an overwhelming number admitted they still felt lonely. They knew the stats. They knew that *the majority of Christian young women are virgins.* (Statistically, over 60 percent are![5]) However, that head knowledge doesn't seem to change the way many of you *feel*. As a result, you dwell on the loneliness that is a very real part of purity. We believe that focusing on the loneliness opens you up to believe the lie that you'll not be able to endure it. And that lie opens you up to compromise.

I (Dannah) know that the *worst* loneliness lies in the aftermath of compromise. When I was fifteen, I was attending a Christian high school. I was active in my youth group and was even identified as a leader and invited to teach the three- to four-year-old Sunday school class at my church.

When I was fifteen, I trained to be a summer missionary who would go into underprivileged neighborhoods to share the gospel. I need you to know that I really loved the Lord, but some powerful lies crept in to temporarily derail where God was leading me.

I was in a Christian dating relationship in which there was great pressure to be sexual. Oh, not to have "sex." But to be sexual. And with each secret act of sin, I convinced myself that it "wasn't really sex." I just *knew* that could never happen to me. After all, I was a Christian girl who believed in purity.

The pressure increased, and things escalated. I knew I needed to break up with this guy, but I

TOP TEN LIST
OF THINGS TO BUST
BOY-CRAZINESS

10 Go on a mission trip.

9 Read *Passion and Purity* by Elisabeth Elliot or *Confessions of a Boy-Crazy Girl* by Paula Hendricks.

8 Begin a journal to your future husband.

7 Write a list of your future husband's qualities.

6 Get a mentor to talk to about it.

5 Exercise or get involved in sports.

4 Invest time in the "man of your life"—your dad!

3 Hang out with friends who aren't boy-crazy.

2 Create a list of great movies and books that don't fuel impure thoughts and romance.

1 Write love letters to God.

couldn't get myself to do it. In crept the lie that "I could not endure the loneliness of purity." So, I did what was to me the unthinkable. I gave away the gift that God meant me to give to my husband on my wedding night.

I can't even begin to tell you how lonely my life became. I quietly resigned from all the ministry positions I loved so dearly. The extra hours in my life created silence for the loneliness to grow. I stayed in that relationship for some time, but a great chasm grew between us. The physical act—which within marriage would have brought us closer—became a gulf between us.

Eventually, I broke up with that guy, but I didn't think there was a single person I could talk to about what had happened—what I had done. Everyone in church seemed so picture perfect. Certainly they never knew the depths of sin that I had. I didn't tell anyone for ten years.

I KNOW WHAT LONELINESS IS. MAYBE YOU DO TOO.

I'm happy to say that by God's grace I fully confessed my sin, and in time the Lord graciously healed up my heart. He gave me a great Christian husband who was a virgin on our wedding night and has extended much forgiveness to me. No, he's *lavished* forgiveness on me. Just like my Savior. And today God is using me to encourage young women like you to choose the pathway of purity. (Our God is so merciful and creative in His restoration of our broken hearts.) If you have known this loneliness, I want you to see the healing in my life and know that God wants this for you too.

 Yes, a commitment to purity challenges you to safeguard your heart until it is the right time to "awaken" love. Yes, this often feels painful, but the pain of self-denial is far better than the pain of self-destruction.

C. S. Lewis, who was a famous Christian author in the 1900s, lost his wife to cancer. The movie *Shadowlands* is about his life and shows Lewis grieving over his wife's illness. As he and his wife reflect on the joy they have experienced together and come to accept her impending death, he remarks, "The pain now is part of the happiness then."[6] It's true. The pain you feel now in the waiting will be the happiness you feel then. It will make your marriage more precious and more beautiful if that is what God has in store for you.

We recognize that waiting can be lonely. We're not saying there won't be days when you wish you had someone to give you flowers or hold you or share life with you. What we are saying is that the long-term reward of oneness with the husband of God's choice will far outweigh the loneliness you feel right now. The measure to which you protect the purity of your future marriage may well impact the measure to which you will experience true intimacy once you are married. Genesis 2:24 promises that you'll be "one flesh" with your husband, if God intends for you to be married someday. Hold on to that promise. The oneness will be worth it.

WE RECOGNIZE THAT WAITING CAN BE LONELY.

I (Nancy) want to add a word for those who struggle with the thought, *What if God doesn't ever give me a husband?* For many single women, the thought of never being married feels like a life sentence—in solitary confinement! Marriage is an incredible gift and I believe God intends for most people to be married. But, having lived as a single woman until my late fifties (when God totally surprised me by bringing an amazing husband into my life), I can assure you that if God's plan is for you to remain single longer than you expected—or even for a lifetime—your life can be as meaningful and blessed as that of any married woman. Yes, there will be challenges (as every married woman faces), but He really will give you daily grace for whatever you may encounter.

THE FACT IS, loneliness is an inescapable reality in a fallen, broken world—whether you're single or married! But if you will set your heart to seek God and His will above anything and anyone else, we can promise that you will never be truly alone, and you will never lack true joy.

DOUSING LIES WITH THE TRUTH

the lie

the truth

It's OK to date whoever I feel like dating.

- God doesn't want you tied to unbelievers. 2 Corinthians 6:14

- Your dating decisions now have huge implications for your future. Job 4:8

- Marriage is designed to be a picture of the oneness of God. Ephesians 5:31

I need a boyfriend.

- The purpose of marriage is not simply to make you happy, but to glorify God. Ephesians 5:31–32

- God does not want you to awaken love until the time is right. Song of Solomon 2:7

It's not really sex.

- Avoid anything that "hints" at sex. Ephesians 5:3

- Exposing yourself to songs, television shows, and movies that use sexual humor "hints" at sexual sin. Ephesians 5:4

- God's standard for purity is high; the rewards are worth the pain of self-control. Philippians 4:13

I can't handle the loneliness of staying pure.

- Abstinence is not about not having sex; it's about waiting to have it right. Deuteronomy 6:24

- A God-honoring marriage, in God's time, is worth every temporary moment of loneliness. Proverbs 3:5–6; Genesis 2:24

[lies young women believe]

making it personal

Perhaps no lies have longer-term consequences and pain than those we believe about guys and sexuality. Don't fall for them. Take some time to answer these questions in your journal:

What lies have I been most likely to believe about guys?

What Scripture verses can I store in my heart to help me counter those lies with the Truth?

Best Youth Leader Ever

I totally don't have any friends!!!!!!!!!!!

WHAT?

I would have so much less anxiety if I had closer friends because then I'd have someone to open up with besides you and Shelly. Something must be wrong with me. If I had friends at school, I wouldn't be so lonely.

In Proverbs there is a verse that says "a man with many friends will come to ruin." If we are constantly chasing after friends, they won't always give the best advice. Maybe we should focus on God instead of getting more "friends"?

Maybe . . .

I bet you're not the only one struggling. Let's talk about this more at youth group tonight. See you at 6!

P. S. Don't forget your camp permission form!

"Wishing to be friends is
a quick work, but friendship
is a slow ripening fruit."

ARISTOTLE

Lies about Relationships

Scene 1: It's ten o'clock on Sunday morning. Sadie bounces from person to person as church is about to begin. She hugs everyone and smiles. She races toward the door when she sees Corrie, the youth pastor's wife, who is planning this weekend's youth retreat. She hugs her and tells her how "psyched" she is for it and that she's really ready for a "God encounter." She thanks her for planning it and races off to hug another needy heart. Sadie has a strong spiritual gift of mercy. She knows it and she loves using it.

Scene 2: It's ten o'clock on Sunday night. Sadie is parked in front of her laptop, where she's been for the last hour. Right now she's messaging Jake. First they talk about how "fake" Corrie is. Then the conversation gets a little sexual. Jake says he'd like to take her virginity away from her, but he's just not sure. After all, she's the pastor's daughter. What would *he* think? Sadie says it's none of her dad's business.

Will the real Sadie please stand up?

Don't know if you've noticed, but relationships seem to be more complex for girls than for guys. Add technology to the equation, and you've got a whole new twist on what it means to be double-faced.

#13 { "It's OK to be one person at home and a different person with others . . . especially online." }

A whopping 84 percent of young women agreed with the statement "I can only be myself around people who are like me, such as friends my own age." This got our attention. We wanted to hear more. The girls we talked to admitted to radical differences between who they are at home and who they are with friends.

Now, to a certain extent that has always been somewhat the angst of teen girls. Yawn! We weren't finding anything new. Then they threw technology into the picture and it got really crazy. It seems quite a few of you have both an at-home persona and an online persona. Well, at least it's true of your "friends." (Wink!)

We asked young women to respond to the statement "I can only be myself around people who are like me, such as friends my own age." Here's what they said:

84% Agree or sometimes agree

16% Disagree

🍎 *I know a lot of people who are one person when you are with them, and they are completely different on Snapchat. I think that they just feel like they have to be something that they are not.*

🍎 *Your good Christian church girls post pictures of themselves that are not explicit but are still sexually suggestive. They believe they can be one thing in person and another person on the computer.*

The longer the conversations went on, the more girls began to admit things about themselves:

🍎 *I would hate it if my mom saw my texts.*

🍎 *When I was in middle school, I actually emailed one girl to say that she should start taking baths because she smelled bad. I can't even believe I did that!*

We found that many professing *Christian* girls we talked to were likely to gossip, use mild to wild profanity, talk casually about things like sex or menstruation with guys, be mean to teens outside of their peer group, and post or look at mild sexual photos when they were online. (Though you'd never dream of doing that at home or at church!) The Internet offers you a place to be someone you are not in person.

What blew us away as we considered this phenomenon is the fact that 71 percent of the young women in the same focus groups also expressed a deep fear of being viewed as hypocritical. They said they despised hypocrisy and didn't want to fall into that category themselves.

At this point, we really need to pull out Webster's! A hypocrite is "a person who acts in contradiction to his or her stated beliefs." Hmmm?

If you claim to act and believe one way in church or at home, but your Snapchats and texts contradict those beliefs, you are being the very thing you said you don't want to be—a hypocrite! We can learn how to keep up appearances pretty well. We know how to look and act when we're at church or trying to make a good impression. But we're called to live lives that can handle close scrutiny—all the time.

If we were to pop on to your social media right now, would it accurately reflect what you claim to believe? What if we could see everything you've sent on Snapchat in the past twenty-four hours? (P.S. You realize those images never really disappear, right?) If we could listen in on your phone calls, would we be able to tell that you're a follower of Christ? Are you texting nasty comments about a friend behind her back?

The Pharisees of Jesus' day *looked* holy. But Jesus said, "You are like whitewashed tombs, which outwardly appear beautiful, . . . but within you are full of hypocrisy and lawlessness" (Matthew 23:27–28).

Jesus despises hypocrisy. He showed kindness and compassion for those who were caught in sin, while He sternly rebuked the religious hypocrites of His day.

Living a life of hypocrisy can have disastrous consequences. That's what happened to one young college-aged woman, who we'll call Carissa. She started out innocently meeting people on the Internet and chatting. But soon she was having intense sexual conversations with them. When that wasn't enough, she began meeting guys in

FIVE WAYS
TO CULTIVATE
AUTHENTIC
FAITH

1

Invite your youth pastor's wife to follow you on Instagram.

2

Text at least one godly word of encouragement to a friend each day.

3

Use your blog as a place for prayer requests and praise reports.

4

Put your favorite verse as your Instagram avatar.

5

Create a board of your favorite Christian books and start pinning!

person. Eventually, she was willing to do things with them that she would never have dreamed of doing just a few months earlier.

Her mother describes Carissa as "sweet" and "compliant" until she was nineteen, when her problems on the Internet began. The family intervened, and Carissa seemed to be responding well. She eventually thanked her mother for the "Truth you poured into me for all those years."

But Carissa was still in bondage. Her mother cried as she shared what has taken place in her daughter's life recently:

Carissa met a woman who was a total stranger and before the afternoon was over they exchanged phone numbers. The woman took Carissa's picture with her cellphone and emailed it to a male acquaintance. Carissa and the young man immediately started a "hot and heavy" texting exchange that led to her meeting him for dinner and then going to his home afterward.

Carissa began a relationship with this guy that, to say the least, was inappropriate. Her life veered terribly out of control, beginning with her willingness to live one life in front of her church friends and family . . . and another on the Internet.

Rather than being hypocritical, God wants you to be single-minded. He wants you to have a faith that is genuine and that is lived out in every arena of your life and relationships. "Draw near to God," the Scripture says, "and he will draw near to you. Cleanse your hands, you sinners, and purify your hearts, you double-minded" (James 4:8). According to James 1:8, a double-minded person is "unstable in all his ways." If you claim to follow Christ while also catering to the world and your flesh, your whole life will become unstable.

At the beginning of the chapter, we introduced you to Sadie. Sadie was clearly a double-minded young woman. And she hated it. The climb back was difficult and tearful. Her parents found some of her text messages and realized she was having sexual conversations with Jake. They took away all her technology privileges and confronted the guy *and* his parents and his youth pastor. It was messy!

But the Lord used the pain to soften her heart, and she went to her Christian high school chaplain to confess and get spiritual help. The chaplain taught her what the Bible says about confessing sin, held her accountable, and helped her return to a place of single-minded devotion to Christ. Today she is living as an authentic Christian who has a whole heart toward God.

God set her free from her hypocrisy and the destruction it could have wreaked in her life.

Does He need to do that for you? If so, make this your prayer: *"Unite my heart to fear your name"* (Psalm 86:11).

#14 "If I just had friends, I wouldn't be so lonely."

You might be saying, "But it's true! I *don't* have any friends." It may be true that you're not the most popular girl at school, you don't have a best friend, or you are even a target of mean girls. In fact, we would bet that you likely struggle with friendship on some level. It is one of the universal girl growing pains. And, oh, the emotion a scorned girlfriend suffers. Who hasn't thrown themselves onto their bed, curled up in a ball, and cried after a really bad friend day?

🍎 *Last week I came home one night and cried for like an hour and a half because I just don't feel like I have a friend at school. I feel like everyone else is in pairs and that I just kind of float from pair to pair as the third wheel. I just don't see how I fit in.*

🍎 *I'm lonely every day. My two best friends just fell apart last year. Both of them experienced their parents' divorce in about a six-month time frame and totally lost it. One dropped out of school altogether. The other transferred. No one really asks me to sit with them or anything.*

My (Dannah's) friend Suzy Weibel captures the roller-coaster ride of girlfriend problems in her book *Secret Diary Unlocked.* In the book she shares actual excerpts from her seventh- and eighth-grade diary. (The high school girls I've spoken to can't put the book down because it sounds just like *their* middle school diary.) You just have to peek into the girlfriend chapter with us. Here are a few of her entries:[1]

December 22: Beth got me a really flip-out mirror with "You're Gorgeous" on it (since I'm always putting myself down).

January 14: I don't think Beth's ("You're Gorgeous") mirror is helping my complex any. It keeps shattering when I go to the Roller Dome. I know I'm not ugly but there's something about me people don't like . . .

January 31: All of a sudden everyone's best friend is Kim . . . suddenly she's the in thing. I guess I'm really jealous. I know I am.

March 7: I don't think Kim likes me. She sure doesn't act like it. She likes Ginny, though. After all I did for Cam in art yesterday, she's back to her "Sue, you're such a dummy" attitude.

If these thoughts sound like the same ones you had in seventh grade, welcome to the club. Though things tend to settle down a bit in high school, the angst of friendship usually continues at some level.

We want to be clear about one thing: your emotions concerning friends are common. They are not in and of themselves bad or sinful. The danger is when we allow our actions and decisions to be controlled by our emotions rather than God's Truth. What is God's Truth about friendship?

FIRST, He created you to know Him and to be His friend.

You may recall that when we dealt with Lie #1, "God is not enough," we commented that friends seemed to be a girl's number one rival for God! The seventeenth-century French philosopher Blaise Pascal wrote that each of us is created with a God-shaped hole within us. We spend an awful lot of our lives trying to fill that empty space with other things, but it's futile—like trying to fill the ocean with a thimble!

The Bible says that Abraham was a friend of God (James 2:23). Jesus says that we are His friends when we know Him and obey His Word (John 15:14). We were created for fellowship with the God of the universe. During their middle school and high school years, a lot of girls tend to try to fill that hole with friends. (Actually, it's not just teens—

> ## EACH OF US IS CREATED WITH A GOD-SHAPED HOLE WITHIN US.
> BLAISE PASCAL

this is a struggle for women of all ages!) But friends can never satisfy the deepest longings and needs of our hearts. Only God can fill that void.

SECOND, there's no greater friend than God. Wouldn't you love to have a friend who:

 never leaves (Hebrews 13:5)

 knows every detail about you . . . (Matthew 10:30)

. . . and, loves you still (John 3:16)

and no matter how tough things get, you'll never be separated from that love (Romans 8:35)

desires to live with you forever (2 John 2)

Now, that's friendship! So why do we spend so much emotional energy desperately pursuing earthly friendships that can never compare? Christie Friedrick is a young woman who says that when she was a teen her best friend was—hands down—God. Often, rather than going out with friends, she spent time with the Lord. (Reminds us of a friend we spoke about who overcame her boy-craziness by spending time with God.) She learned early to cultivate her friendship with God. Just as we have to spend time with a friend to grow closer, so we must spend time with God. It's not so He'll get to know us better, but so we'll get to know Him and trust His friendship.

Once you fill that God-sized hole with the only One who is big enough to fill it, you'll never look at friendship the same again. The friendships you do have will be added blessings, but not desperate necessities.

There's one more thing we feel we need to address in regard to friendship. A lot of what we heard from the girls in our research was . . . well . . . can we say it like it is? It was selfish. You may need to take a different approach to your earthly friendships.

You are called to be a true friend. If your focus is on who likes you, you're not pursuing true friendship. If your focus is on who is asking *you* to hang with *them*, it's all wrong. That's not a spiritual mindset. Ask the Lord to help you be more concerned about who *needs* you than who *likes* you.

A friend should show herself friendly and shouldn't be overly concerned with quantity of friends, but with the depth of friendship (Proverbs 18:24). A friend loves all the time and will be there through thick and thin—divorces, sickness, and school transfers (Proverbs 17:17). Friends don't use flattery or smooth words. Instead, they are truthful even if it means inflicting temporary wounds (Proverbs 27:6).

There are people who need your friendship. Ask God to give you eyes to see who they are and start becoming a friend today. And please, please, please—if it's not too late—don't do that silly, superficial girl thing around seventh or eighth grade where you cut off every friend who is not as old as you. If you can just *be* a friend through the next few awkward months, you might *have* a friend for life.

Let's go back to my (Dannah's) friend, author Suzy Weibel. She was speaking at a youth event once where a girl came up to her desperate for friends. This girl truly seemed to be the target of mean girls. Suzy counseled her that her best friend, other than Jesus, might just be a good book or a furry four-legged creature. But she also challenged her to stop wanting someone to befriend her and to start looking for someone to befriend. A few weeks later, the girl emailed Suzy saying:

I took your advice. I reached out to a girl who sits alone at lunch each day. She's actually pretty cool. We're becoming fast friends. Turns out she needed a friend, and I just needed to be one.

Want some good Truth about friendship? The Truth is that you are called to be a true friend to others in need and to experience friendship with Christ.

#15 { "I'm my own authority." }

Have you ever had a conversation with your mom that went something like this:

MOM: Honey, it's time to leave. I gave you a ten-minute warning. Please come downstairs.

YOU: Mom! I don't have to be there for fifteen more minutes! Gosh!

Mom: It takes fifteen minutes to get there. Please come get your shoes on.

YOU: (Coming out into the hallway) Look! Do you see my hair? It's a mess! YOU should have gotten me up earlier so I could take a shower. My hair is disgusting! I can't go like this! Pleeaaase! (Stomping off to the bathroom.)

MOM: You have sixty seconds. Bring your stuff with you. You can pull your hair back in the car.

YOU: (Stomping down the stairs.) You just don't understand. You never do. What's wrong with you? (Slamming door to the house.)

A bestselling secular book on raising girls suggests that this conversation should be considered a high compliment to the mother. After all, the author says, the daughter is allowing the mother into her inner hurt, and that's a good thing. She knows that her mother, being a woman, understands. According to this author, the mother just needs to weather such interactions and learn to take the compliment.[2]

We beg to differ! We say that conversation reveals a spirit of rebellion and disrespect and shouldn't take place in any Christian home. But we bet it sounds awfully familiar! How could we guess? Well, we don't have surveillance cameras in your house, so it must just be that we've seen some of that in our own homes.

Satan hates authority and has given you and me a special distaste for it as well. The struggle to submit is not unique to our day and age. In fact, that was the essence of the issue Eve faced back in the garden of Eden. At the heart of the Serpent's approach to Eve was the challenge, "Does God have the right to rule your life?" Satan said, in effect, "You can run your own life; you don't have to submit to anyone else's authority."

> **EVEN WHEN YOU DO NOT AGREE with the AUTHORITY GOD has placed over you, love and respect for Christ should MOTIVATE YOU to submit.**

He convinced Eve that if she submitted to God's direction, she would be miserable and would miss out on something in life. From that day to this, Satan has done a masterful job of convincing women that submission is a negative, confining concept. He uses our culture, the ever-growing prominence of psychology, and Hollywood entertainment to fuel our rebellion. Apparently some of you see it as clearly as we do. The majority of young women we spoke to admitted that they act in accordance with the lie "I'm my own authority." Some communicated the conflict like this:

 I think that a lot of times today's media, especially movies, depict parents as dumb or like they don't have a clue or that they are weird. The media wants us to perceive them as if they are not a person, like they are just a stupid authority that doesn't have a clue.

 Fighting with your parents is no big deal.

The rebellious thing is always the cool thing to do for every generation.

Satan has been ruining families, friendships, and marriages for centuries through rebellion. His arsenal of lies about submission is endless. Let's disarm a few of those **LIES** before we look at the Truth.

I only need to submit if I agree with my authority. That's not submission. That's just agreement and cooperation. Ephesians 5:21 says we are to submit to God-ordained authority "out of reverence for Christ." Even when you do not agree with the authority God has placed over you, love and respect for Christ should motivate you to submit.

I can't express my thoughts or opinions to my authority. Submitting doesn't mean you can't think. In some instances you can even express your different ideas if you do it with a humble, respectful attitude. That *doesn't* give you the freedom to raise your voice, stomp around, or disobey if your authority does not change his or her mind.

My authority is always right. That's the thing about submission. Sometimes your parents, teachers, pastor, or government leaders will be wrong. They are human, after all. You can expect that sometimes they will make bad decisions. (Check out the sidebar on the following page for some advice on what to do when you think they're wrong.) Even then, your act of submission will be a form of protection. So . . . what's the **TRUTH** about submission?

How to **Respond to Parents** When You **Don't Agree** with Their Decisions

➡ **We recognize that not every girl reading this book has perfect parents.** (Hmmm. Let's try that again!) We recognize that no one has perfect parents. So, how do you respond when you feel they're being unreasonable, or that their decisions are even wrong? Here are some suggestions.

➡ **Remember that every human authority ultimately answers to God and that God is big enough to change your parents' hearts if that is needed** (Proverbs 21:1). Learn to trust in God and His sovereign plan; remember that He is able to override any mistakes your parents could make.

➡ **Check your attitude and ask forgiveness for any wrongdoing on your part.** Ask God to show you if you are being stubborn, rebellious, or disrespectful in any way. If you've been guilty of pride, grumbling, or stomping around, and you confess your bad attitude to your parents, it will go a long way in your parents feeling like they can trust you. (They may also be willing to acknowledge their own mistakes.)

➡ **Invest in your relationship with your parents.** When was the last time you wrote your mom or dad a note, invited them to go out for ice cream, or offered to help with chores around the house? If you let them know you're interested in them, communication will likely improve and problems will be easier to solve.

➡ **Talk to the Lord about it.** Ask Him to change your parents' hearts if they are wrong. Ask Him to give you grace to respond with the right heart attitude and wisdom to know the right thing to do in the circumstance. Then give Him time to work in both your lives.

➡ **Make an appeal.** That's what Daniel did when the king ordered him to eat food he knew God didn't want him to eat. He respectfully proposed an alternative plan. The king granted his appeal, and God protected Daniel from having to make a sinful choice (Daniel 1:5–16). Respectfully ask your parents if they would be willing to make a different decision. Unless what they are asking you to do is sinful, let them know you will submit to their authority, regardless of what they decide.

➡ **Choose to obey** your parents, even when you disagree with them, unless they require you to do something that is forbidden in the Scriptures or prohibit you from doing something that Scripture commands. Remember that even Jesus, who was the sinless Son of God, was once a teenager and had to deal with obeying His earthly parents. They were sinful and sometimes made mistakes, but He still obeyed them (Luke 2:51).

Submission places you under God's protection. Rebellion opens you up to the influence of Satan in ways you may not even realize. When we place ourselves under the spiritual covering of the authorities God has placed in our lives, God protects us. (That doesn't mean nothing bad or hard will ever happen to us, but that He will walk with us through every problem.) On the other hand, when we insist on having it our way and stepping out from under that protection, we become vulnerable and give the Enemy a new opportunity to attack us.

SUBMISSION places you under God's PROTECTION.

We believe that the failure of many Christian young women to place themselves under their parents', teachers', and pastors' authority is one reason some of you are suffering the Enemy's attack on your mind, will, and emotions. It also establishes a pattern for you to disrespect and rebel against your husband's authority if you are ever married one day.

I (Dannah) struggled with respecting my husband for nearly ten years of my marriage before I learned how beautiful it could be if I would choose to honor Bob. Oh, I never rebelled in big things. If he asked me to move across the country, I would. But all chaos broke loose if he tried to decide small things for us—like where to park at church or when to leave for the airport. Stupid stuff! I know! My dear husband was amazingly loving, patient, and kind. I, on the other hand, was frequently bossy, snappy, and cold. (Brings back memories of how I was with my mom when I was a teenager.)

One day the Lord let me see it all from His eyes. I literally woke my husband up in the middle of the night to apologize for how I'd wounded our marriage in this way. From that day on, our marriage truly blossomed. Though it may have seemed I gave up control to Bob, I believe I was ultimately giving up control to God. And He was able to make my marriage beautiful.

ON THE SURFACE, submitting to your parents and other authorities is about your relationship with them, but in the unseen realm it is about a bigger battle for control—will you submit your will to God, or are you going to insist on being your own authority? When you are willing to obey Him, you'll find that it is not nearly so difficult to submit to your mom, your dad, or your teacher.

[lies young women believe]

WHAT IT COMES DOWN TO IS THIS: **Our willingness to submit to human authorities is an evidence of how big we believe God really is.** Do you believe He is bigger and greater than any human authority? Do you trust that He is big enough to change the hearts of those He has placed in authority over you? Proverbs 21:1 assures us that "the king's heart is a stream of water in the hand of the LORD; he turns it wherever he will."

The Truth about submission is that a higher authority controls every human authority and that godly submission is a means of great blessing and protection.

the lie

the truth

It's OK to be one person at home and a different person in public . . . especially online.

• If your life contradicts what you say you believe, you are a hypocrite. Matthew 23:27b–28

• God wants you to be single-minded and stable. James 1:8; 4:8

If I just had friends, I wouldn't be so lonely.

• You are called to be a true friend. Proverbs 18:24; Proverbs 17:17

• You are called to pursue friendship with Christ. John 15:13–15

I'm my own authority.

• Submission places you under the protection of God. Ephesians 5:21

• Rebellion opens you up to the attack of Satan. 1 Samuel 15:23

• Your willingness to put yourself under God-ordained authority is the greatest evidence of how big you believe God is. Proverbs 21:1

making it personal

Relationships are a great gift from God if we receive them in a healthy way, but lies about relationships can make relationships painful. Stop the cycle of hurt in your life by choosing to pursue Truth. Grab your journal and answer these questions:

What lies have I been most likely to believe about relationships?

What Scripture verses can I store in my heart to help me counter those lies with the Truth?

CallieBug

Did you hear that Pastor Matt is leaving???? 🙁

Why would he leave us?! He is the one person I tell everything to!!!! Why would God do this?!?!

Whatev! Pastor Matt is SO not God! He is SO not perfect like God is. He obviously does not have all of the answers . . . and God will never abandon you. You need to chill! #forreals

Maybe God is calling Pastor Matt to a new place in order to help another kid like he helped you!

...

"All too often what passes for Christianity is not true Christianity at all. It is an imposter. And the sad thing is that most people don't know the difference."

J. DAVID HOKE

Lies about My Faith

On the morning we began writing this chapter, I (Dannah) met with Courtney at Starbucks. Courtney is the daughter of a church elder. Her mom is in leadership for their church's children's ministry. Her family is actively devoted to the Christian faith. Our conversation about the body of Christ went something like this:

Dannah: Today I'm going to write about lies about church. This is the area where we saw the most emotion in girls around the nation. A lot of tears were shed.

Courtney: Really? Why?

Dannah: Mostly about youth pastors.

Courtney: Why would girls cry about youth pastors?

Dannah: Because they leave.

Courtney's eyes become wide, and she nods her head in total agreement.

Courtney: Yes, you have to write about that! That happened to my church. The youth pastor had an affair, and one day he was just gone. One girl could never get over it. Of course, she was over-the-top connected to him. Her email address was "PCslittleangel"—"Pastor Chad's little angel." She cried when he left and was angry

---

WILL MY YOUTH PASTOR **LEAVE**?

The average youth worker stays at the same church for 3.9 years. Most teens experience at least one youth pastor turnover during their middle school and high school years.[1]

---

at the leaders for making him leave. He didn't even apologize for his sin. He tried to justify it. Anyway, this girl stopped coming to church. She never did get over it.

Dannah: How long did it take your youth group to get over it?

Courtney: It still hasn't.

Pastor "Chad" left five years ago. Since then, Courtney's youth group has had another youth pastor whom the leadership asked to leave for not doing his job well. They're just now introducing another one.

Dannah: Are you active in your youth group?

Courtney: Not really.

Dannah: Why?

Courtney: I think my youth group is a joke.

Dannah: Does it have anything to do with your youth pastor's leaving so abruptly?

Courtney: It has everything to do with that.

#16 { "My youth pastor is my connection to God." }

This lie was unquestionably the one that evoked the most tears in our focus groups. And the fact is, humanly speaking, you may be justified in your disappointment. Many of you have watched one or more youth pastors leave. And many times they do not leave gracefully. Even if they do, you may feel abandoned by someone who has been a significant advisor in your spiritual life.

 I know youth pastors change their jobs all of the time, but that is terrible to me. My youth pastor was the person in my life that I told everything to, and when that was taken away, I didn't know what to do.

My church is the biggest in town, and my youth pastor seems to be so discontent here. It's like this is just a stopping place on his journey.

People experience their youth pastors and think of them as God. We see them as holy, and maybe that's why they don't stay. God knows how dangerous it is when we start looking to other people instead of Him. In your head you know that they are not God, but when they leave you are like . . . "Oh my!" . . . and you don't realize that God is still there.

Your youth pastors and leaders are important spiritual leaders in your life, *but we have access to God through Christ and Christ alone.*
Bible scholars call this "the priesthood of believers" (see 1 Peter 2:9). In Old Testament times, God appointed certain men as priests. They led the people of Israel in worship and offered prayers and sacrifices on behalf of God's people. Today, Christ is our High Priest. By His death on the cross, He made a complete sacrifice for our sin and invites us to come directly into God's presence through our relationship with Him. "There is one mediator between God and men, the man Christ Jesus, who gave himself as a ransom for all" (1 Timothy 2:5–6).

When a spiritual leader leaves or wounds you, you have an opportunity to draw closer to Christ and to let Him heal you with His grace.

Sadly, many of you confessed that your experiences with youth pastors leaving have caused you to withdraw from church and sometimes from God. One young woman said,

 I think it is why a lot of people don't ever return to church after they leave high school.

It's probably not *the* reason, but after talking with hundreds of you we are convinced that it is *a* reason that many don't return to church after their parents no longer require it. I (Dannah) understand completely the temptation to withdraw from church when your youth pastor wounds you. When I was in junior high school, I had a terrific youth pastor; he made a significant impact on my life during a crucial season. As I became an adult, we didn't stay in touch, but I would get tapes of his sermons mailed to me. I greatly revered him—maybe *too* much. Years later, when I was in my early *thirties,* he lashed out against me in a painful way. Looking back, I realize that he had some justifiable concerns, but in the process of addressing them he cut me off from other friends and advisors.

I was emotionally devastated! This was my youth pastor! The man who'd mentored me through the two toughest years of my life—seventh and eighth grades. How could he hurt me like this? I came to realize that I'd placed him on a pedestal years earlier and that he was still sitting there.

My natural reaction was to want to stop going to church even though I was no longer in his church. For several months, I only went to church out of obedience. It took me two years to fully recover. Sometime later, this former youth pastor came to me and apologized for the way he handled things. I really believe the Lord wanted to teach me a lesson about not elevating spiritual leaders to a place that should be reserved only for God.

Having been through this experience, *I understand your hurt*! Still, you can't blame anyone for the choices you make about church. *We are each accountable for our own actions and reactions.* You can't blame your youth pastor for any choice you may make to disconnect from the body of Christ.

God's family works best together! You need them, and they need you. No matter how many bad experiences you may have in church—and we know you will have them because Satan hates the church and is always attacking it—the best place for you to grow, serve, and be discipled is in a local church body.

The first church body met together regularly and shared everything they had. They met one another's physical needs; they were committed to one another; they stuck together and provided spiritual support for one another through thick and thin. They weren't perfect, and neither is any church today. But the church is God's plan; Jesus loves it and gave His life for it. It may be tempting to cut yourself off when the going gets tough, but as a part of God's spiritual family, He hasn't given us the option of "dropping out."

#17 { "Everyone at church is judging me." }

This was one of our whopper lies. Ninety-one percent of the girls in our focus groups agreed that they always or sometimes felt judged. Only 9 percent of them felt that the churches they attended did not have people who judged them. This great fear of being judged manifested in two powerful ways that we think are dangerous.

FIRST, many tended to feel pressure to be fake.

🍎 *I'm afraid to fall into a stereotype. I know that if I don't worship a certain way or share a lot, people aren't going to understand that my faith is real. But, I don't want to do what they want me to do just because they want me to do it. I want to express my faith in a way that's comfortable for me. I don't want fake Christianity.*

🍎 *There are a lot of people who expect me to be just like them.*

SECOND, many said they were less likely to tell someone older about sin they were struggling with, for fear of being judged. It seems the vast majority of young women have never experienced the blessing of someone helping them overcome their sin.

🍎 *I sit in the pews every week and see all these picture-perfect families. My sin is pretty ugly. I want so badly to have someone to talk to, but I know that's not possible.*

🍎 *A support group for alcoholics meets at our church on Sundays right before we come back for evening activities. You should have heard the uproar when that decision was made. They're not the cleanest bunch. They smoke in the parking lot, and that really ruffled some feathers. Here's a group of people being real about their need, and the one place that's supposed to welcome them—the place that has the Answer—is too busy fighting over whether they should meet here or not. Do you think I'd ever talk about my sin? No way!*

JUDGMENTAL **JURIES**

We asked young women to agree or disagree with the statement "I feel everyone at church is judging me." Here's how they responded:

91% Always or sometimes agree

9% Never agree

Humanly speaking, we can understand that reaction. We're told not to judge by mere appearances (John 7:24). And that when we have a judgmental spirit, we can count on being judged more severely ourselves (Matthew 7:1–2).

When you see and hear Christians having a judgmental spirit, you should respond by being kind but truthful. Something like, "I know those people are smoking, but it seems to me that they're trying to get help and are headed in the right direction. What they really need is Jesus. Let's pray that they find Him here."

But what if the judgment is directed at you? What do you do then? You might be surprised to hear that we think you should respond with a humble heart to those who are judging you. Let's say that you show up to church in the fab outfit you just bought during your all-day Saturday shopping spree! You found it irresistibly adorable. You were sure to put it through every modesty test you know before you put out the cash for it.

"Yes," you said to yourself. "This is cute and modest! Definite good church-wear!"

Cha-ching! Sold!

But here you are at church looking all "cute and modest" when an older, godly woman you know approaches you. She happens to be the children's ministry director, and she knows you teach the three- and four-year-olds. She's not really looking so cute on this day.

When did that outfit go out of style, anyway? you think to yourself. *Oh, well, she sure is modest.*

Apparently, she doesn't think your outfit is all that modest and, though she is kind, she doesn't waste time in telling you so. In fact, she asks you to run home to change before you teach the three- and four-year-old class.

Your heart drops!

You have no idea what to say.

You could see yourself running into the bathroom to cry, but that would be even more embarrassing. Then, maybe it'd be better to stomp off to say a thing or two about Miss Much-Too-Modest.

TIME OUT!

The issue really isn't so much who's right or who's wrong. The issue is that you and I are called to honor and esteem others in the body of Christ. The Word of God actually challenges us to "outdo one another in showing honor" (Romans 12:10) and to "show proper respect to everyone" (1 Peter 2:17 NIV).

So what do you do in this situation?

How about something radical? Like—you ask your mom for the car keys and suggest that it might be a good idea for you to go home and change in the break between morning worship and Sunday school. In this way you would honor your supervisor. There are times when we are called to simply, quietly *defer* to the preferences of others.

IS IT JUDGMENT OR DISCIPLINE?

Be careful not to confuse judgment with discipline. Sin clearly places any believer in a position to be disciplined (Hebrews 12:7–11; Matthew 18:15–17). We recognize that some churches may lack grace and thoroughness in the discipline process. We wish that were not the case. However, if someone in your congregation sins, he should be disciplined, with the goal that he will repent and be restored.

[lies young women believe]

It's natural to become defensive or resistant when we feel criticized or judged. But the ability to respond in humility is a sign of maturity. We can actually learn a lot from our critics if we respond to them with a humble, teachable attitude.

All that said, after talking with many of you we feel confident that a lot of what you are experiencing is not *actual* judgment but the *fear* of being judged. Let us say that one more time in a different way. Most of what you are experiencing is in your head! Actually, let's say it again. OK, not really, but you get the point.

DE·FER
(de -fûr') v.
To submit to the opinion, wishes, or decision of another through respect or in recognition of his or her authority, knowledge, or judgment.
Synonym: yield.[2]

We believe that most of the time you're not actually being judged; you're just *afraid* of it. This was brought home as we realized that some of the teens in our own churches and ministries felt afraid of *our* judgment. The fact is, we love them like crazy, and there's nothing they could tell us that would throw us for a loop. We might not agree with some of their choices, and we would love them enough to be honest with them if we felt they were walking contrary to the Truth (we would want them to do the same for us!). But that would not diminish our commitment and our love for them one iota!

The fear of being judged can cause you to withdraw from sources of mature wisdom, especially when it comes to confessing sin you need help in overcoming. James 5:16 says, "Confess your sins to one another and pray for one another, that you may be healed." While it's true that Christ has made it possible for us to go directly to God for forgiveness, it is also true that confessing our sin to each other is important. You'll find so much healing in sharing your secret shame with someone who can wrap her arms around you and love you and help you walk through the issue in a biblical way. (You may even find that she's been there herself!)

It's not easy to share your sins with someone older and wiser and ask her to pray for you. But if you will humble yourself and overcome your fear of being judged, you will experience the blessing of finding release from both the sin in your life as well as that nasty fear of judgment.

#18 { "Of course I'm a Christian, I . . ." }

For many years, I (Nancy) have been deeply concerned about people who have grown up in the church and claim to be Christians, even though there is little if any evidence in their lives of true salvation. They have been deceived into believing various forms of this lie.

"OF COURSE	I'm a Christian; I go to church all the time."
"OF COURSE	I'm a Christian; my parents are."
"OF COURSE	I'm a Christian; I grew up in the church."
"OF COURSE	I'm a Christian; I went forward at church camp!"
"OF COURSE	I'm a Christian; my mom told me that I prayed to receive Christ when I was three."

The list goes on and on.

But the essence of true salvation is not a matter of profession or performance; rather, it is a transformation. Only God can truly tell if someone is a believer, but He's given us some standards by which we can judge ourselves. For starters, 2 Corinthians 5:17 says: *"If anyone is in Christ, he is a new creation. The old has passed away; behold, the new has come."* The person who has been "born again" has a new life, a new heart, a new nature, a new allegiance, a new Master. Have you ever experienced that kind of radical change in your life?

The first epistle of John was written to provide assurance of salvation to those who

HOW DO **AMERICAN TEENS** BELIEVE YOU GET TO **HEAVEN**?

53% A personal relationship with Jesus Christ

27% Acts of kindness

26% Religion[3]

Jesus said, "I am the way, and the truth, and the life. No one comes to the Father except through me" (John 14:6). There is one way to heaven, and it is through turning from sin and confessing your faith in Jesus Christ as your personal Lord and Savior. Have you taken that step of faith and surrender?

had been genuinely converted—and to warn those who had no real basis for their profession of salvation. John identifies specific characteristics that distinguish between those who have been truly saved and those who profess to be saved but are merely religious hypocrites. Here are some of the characteristics he pinpoints:

They obey GOD'S commands

"And by this we know that we have come to know him, if we keep his commandments. Whoever says " I know him" but does not keep his commandments is a liar, and the truth is not in him . . ."

They act like Jesus

"By this we may know that we are in him: whoever says he abides in him ought to walk in the same way in which he walked."

They don't hold grudges (aka No mean girls!)

"Whoever says he is in the light and hates his brother is still in darkness."

They don't have to see every movie and TV show and have every new song the world offers

"If anyone loves the world, the love of the Father is not in him."

They don't wander away from their faith

"For if they had been of us, they would have continued with us. But they went out, that it might become plain that they all are not of us."

(1 John 2:3–4, 5–6, 9, 15, 19)

Growing up in a Christian family can be a great blessing, but it does not make you a Christian. Being active in your youth group does not make you a Christian; nor does attending Christian school or praying a prayer or being a "good girl."

Only a true encounter with Jesus Christ—in which the Holy Spirit convicts you of your sin and draws you to Christ, and you respond in repentance and faith—establishes you as a member of God's family. Nothing apart from this act of free grace on the part of God can make you a Christian. There is nothing *you* can *do* on your own to become a Christian (Ephesians 2:8–9).

As soon as you respond to God's love and give your life to Him, the Holy Spirit comes to live within you. He makes you a new person and gives you a new heart to want to obey and serve Him. He also gives you the desire and the power to resist sin and to do good works that glorify God. That transformation was beautifully illustrated in a girl that I (Dannah) first talked with at an old '50s diner located near her college campus.

Tish had emailed me, confessing that she was breaking up with yet another guy she'd had sex with. She was perplexed that she couldn't seem to overcome sexual sin in spite of the fact that she grew up in the church and had remained actively involved. Her recurring sin left her feeling abandoned and emotionally bloodied after every relationship.

As we sat and talked, tears streamed down her face. The pain was so real. It seemed that she had tried everything to overcome this. Prayer. Bible reading. Lots of boundaries in her dating. Still, she always failed.

At one point in the conversation, the

AN ETERNAL PRAYER

Dear God,

I confess that I have sinned. I understand that my sin is ultimately rebellion against You, and it blocks me from having a relationship with You. Please forgive me. I believe that Jesus Christ is Your Son who died on the cross to take the punishment for my sin. I want to accept this free gift and turn from my sin. I know I cannot overcome it on my own. Send Your Holy Spirit to dwell in me so I can have victory over sin and live a life that is pleasing to You. When I die, take me to live with You in heaven. Until then, help me to serve You and honor You.

In the Name of Jesus,

Amen

[lies young women believe]

Lord brought to mind the New Testament story of Nicodemus. Let me tell you, given this girl's history in the church, I felt a little silly even bringing up such a familiar story.

"Tish," I began. "I know this will probably sound really elementary, but I feel like God wants me to read a story from the Bible to you."

"OK," she stammered. Her eyes continued to water as I read the account of Nicodemus, a leader in the religious Jewish system, sneaking off into the night to ask Jesus how to get into heaven. Jesus said that he needed to be born again—of the Spirit of God.

"Tish," I continued. "If a guy like Nicodemus could go through his entire life as a leader in the Jewish 'church' but still not have a relationship with the One who loved him, I have to wonder if a college woman could have the same predicament."

Tears flowed even more freely now.

"Do you want to be born again?" I asked.

"Yes," she answered. And we prayed together.

Through the years, others had planted many seeds in her heart along the way. But this was her moment of salvation. In that moment of simply trusting Christ to save her and relinquishing control of her life to Him, she received His Holy Spirit who would give her the power to fight temptation and to begin living a life pleasing to God.

That was seven years ago. Tish is still single, and even though she's had a few significant relationships since then, sex has not been a part of those relationships. She is walking in moral freedom and is serving the Lord by working with students at a church in Pennsylvania. She's been on multiple mission trips and is a completely different young woman!

Your background may be similar to Tish's—or the details may be quite different. The question is: **Have you ever come to the point Tish came to? Have you realized that by your sin, you've actually been rebelling against God? Have you confessed your sin to Him? And have you surrendered control of your life to Him?**

 As we'll see in the next chapter, becoming a Christian doesn't mean that overnight you become a spiritual giant or that you never struggle with temptation again. But when you experience what the Bible calls being "born again," you become an entirely different person and begin the incredible journey for which God created you!

DOUSING LIES WITH THE TRUTH

the lie

My youth pastor is my connection to God.

Everyone at church is judging me.

Of course I'm a Christian, I . . .

the truth

• We have access to God only through Jesus Christ.
1 Peter 2:9; Hebrews 13:15–16

• You need the church and the church needs you. 1 Corinthians 12:12–27; Hebrews 10:24–25

• We are to show honor and deference to others, even those we may feel are judging us.
Romans 12:14–21

• Our fear of being judged can never be an excuse to hide sin.
James 5:16

• There is nothing we can do to earn our relationship with God.
Ephesians 2:8–9

• True conversion requires faith in Christ as Savior and Lord and will be accompanied by a growing love for God, a growing hatred for sin, and a growing desire to obey God's Word.
Romans 10:9–10; Acts 20:21

• If you are a child of God, there will be evidence that you are a new person, including the power to overcome sin and to obey God. 2 Corinthians 5:17

[lies young women believe]

making it personal

While lies about our faith are one of Satan's old tools, he's just customized them in new ways for your generation. Why not grab your journal and start to feast on some Truth about the body of Christ? Focus on these questions as you write:

What lies have I been most likely to believe about my faith?

What Scripture verses can I store in my heart to help me counter those lies with the Truth?

Ashbodash

got a present for ya!

for real?

Yeah . . . it's a pirated copy of that movie you've been dying to see. It just releases in theatres this week, but I've got a digital download with your name on it!!!!

Isn't that like breaking the law or something?

I do it for my friends all the time . . . it's not that big a deal . . . the people who make those movies have PLENTY of money. We don't have to waste our $$$ to buy overpriced movie tickets.

I guess if you think you can break the law and get away with it then there is not much stopping ya, but do me a favor . . . give it to someone else. I'm not cool with that. Wanna go see it in the theatre with me this weekend instead?

"Sin introduces a kind of
static interference in
communication with God
and as a result shuts us off
from the very resources we
need to combat it."

PHILIP YANCEY

Lies about Sin

Once you've placed your faith in Christ and have assurance that you are a child of God, remember that although you are a new creation in Christ, with a new desire to love and serve Him, *Christians aren't perfect*. The initial point of salvation, which the Bible calls our *justification*, is followed by a lifelong process that the Bible calls *sanctification*. That's an important theological word that has to do with becoming more and more like Jesus in every area of your life.

That process takes time. No one goes from being a "baby" to being a "grown-up" overnight—physically or spiritually. The process of spiritual growth has its ups and downs. You will never get to the place where you are immune to temptation or where you do not desperately need His mercy and grace. The Bible describes the Christian life as a battle. Sometimes that battle can be pretty intense and messy.

But you should expect to become more consistently victorious as you mature in your faith. And that may not happen if you are believing lies about sin. Let's see if we can combat those lies with the Truth.

#19 { "I can't overcome my sin." }

So many of you feel it.

➡ The shame.

➡ The guilt.

➡ The ache.

Perhaps you struggle with lying. Or with gossip. Maybe you feel as if you can't control the urge to cheat, though you promise that each time will be the last. Or you may feel imprisoned by a secret sin that no one knows about.

Can we be frank? We know there are young women reading this book who are in bondage to sexual sin—including sexual activity before marriage (fornication), lesbianism, and masturbation. Those are not easy things to talk about (and should never be talked about casually). But so many have come to us pleading for help with these and other issues that we just can't ignore them. These are very real battles, and many young women growing up in a Christian environment are experiencing recurring or chronic defeat in their battle with sin and temptation.

What concerns us so much about this lie is that what you believe determines the way you live. If you believe you are going to sin, then you will. If you believe you have to live in bondage, then you will. If you believe you can't overcome sin, you won't. If you don't overcome this lie with the Truth, you'll have a hard time overcoming many other lies.

Would it surprise you if we started by saying, "You're right—you *can't* overcome sin"? That is, *you* cannot overcome sin. You are powerless to change yourself. "Apart from me," Jesus said, "you can do nothing" (John 15:5). While you cannot overcome sin on your own, Christ can change you. Through His power (and only through His power), you can say no to sin and yes to God.

If you are in Christ, the Truth is:

HAVING BEEN SET FREE FROM SIN, [YOU] HAVE BECOME SLAVES OF RIGHTEOUSNESS. . . . FOR THE LAW OF THE SPIRIT OF LIFE HAS SET YOU FREE IN CHRIST JESUS FROM THE LAW OF SIN AND DEATH. (ROMANS 6:18; 8:2)

He first sets you free when you are born again. Tish, the college-aged girl we wrote about in the last chapter, could not overcome her sexual sin even though she was active in her church and was praying and reading her Bible. She simply couldn't do it because she had never been born again— she was still a slave to sin. She didn't have the power of the Holy Spirit within her to overcome sin, and she was still ruled by her old nature. But when she received Christ as her Savior, that old nature died and she was set free from sin; she now had the power to overcome her habitual sin. Through Christ's death, you and I can do the same.

**We know that our old self was crucified with him
in order that the body of sin might be brought to nothing,
so that we would no longer be enslaved to sin.
For one who has died has been set free from sin.** (Romans 6:6–7)

[lies young women believe]

Anyone who is a true follower of Jesus Christ will begin to have victory over sin. Even the most addictive habits can be overcome through Christ. In some cases, that victory is immediate. Author Becky Tirabassi reported struggling with alcoholism through her teen and college-aged years until she received Christ, at which point she was immediately set free from her compulsion to drink.

However, you may have a genuine relationship with Jesus and still find yourself plagued by a sin that you keep giving in to again and again. God does not immediately deliver us from every sinful compulsion at the point of salvation, as Becky experienced in relation to alcohol. But as children of God, we have the power to overcome every sinful bondage and practice.

YOU CAN SAY NO TO SIN AND YES TO GOD

If you find yourself dealing with the same sinful pattern in your life over and over again, ask yourself a few questions: *Do I truly agree with God that this behavior is sin, or do I secretly think there's really nothing wrong with what I'm doing?* The Bible teaches us that God hates sin because it is rebellion against Him and because it destroys our lives. But *do you hate your sin?* **Have you come to a place where you genuinely long to be free from this sinful pattern in your life?**

God has given us many resources to help us overcome sin: His Holy Spirit, His grace, His Word, and prayer, to name a few. One of the most important resources He has given us is the body of Christ—other believers. Galatians 6:1 says, "Brothers, if anyone is caught in any transgression, you who are spiritual should restore him in a spirit of gentleness." This passage is addressed to *believers*. True believers sometimes get "tripped up" in sin.

We believe that it is impossible to overcome sin in your life without the involvement of others in the body. As we mentioned in the last chapter, there can be enormous value in confessing your sin to an older, wiser person in your local church. **Confiding in someone about your sin can be an important step in the process of your breaking free from that sin.** It will bring you the accountability and prayer power that you need to continue walking in victory.

In my (Nancy's) book titled *Brokenness: The Heart God Revives*, I shared about a battle I faced with a habitual sin when I was in my midtwenties. God's Spirit first began to convict me that I was guilty of "exaggerating the truth" (lying). Here is what I wrote:

Though no one else knew of my deception, and though others might have considered my offenses relatively inconsequential, I experienced an almost suffocating (and blessed!) sense of God's conviction in my heart, and I knew this was something I had to bring into the light.

I agreed with God, confessed my deception, and purposed to begin speaking Truth in every situation. But I soon discovered that lying was a stronghold in my life—it was deeply ingrained. I was hooked and couldn't seem to get free.[1]

God brought the principle of James 5:16 to my mind: "Confess your sins to one another and pray for one another, that you may be healed. The prayer of a righteous person has great power." The Lord prompted me to confess to two godly friends my sin of lying. It was one of the hardest things I'd ever had to do, but that step of humility, along with the accountability and prayers of my friends, was the starting place of my experiencing freedom from the stronghold of lying.

You may have sinful patterns in your life that no one else knows about—perhaps even the same sin of lying that I had to deal with. And if you told someone, you'd be afraid that they would judge you. (There's a double whammy to be tackled here!) You can be free, but you'll most likely need to go through the difficult process of opening your heart to someone you know and respect. This is particularly true of sins of the heart like gossip and lying, where you need nothing more than your own tongue to fall into sin.

Then, if your sin involves something external like a person or your Facebook page, you must pursue "radical amputation" of whatever causes you to sin. Matthew 18:8 reads, "If your hand or your foot causes you to sin, cut it off and throw it away. It is better for you to enter life crippled or lame than with two hands or two feet to be thrown into the eternal fire."

HIS POINT? If something is causing you to sin, get rid of it! If your computer is a portal to sin, shut it down. If you find yourself consistently sinning in a certain relationship, cut it off. If you are tempted to send provocative pictures through Snapchat, shut your account down. It's pretty basic. Stop giving yourself access to the things that lead you into sin, and you'll kill the heart of the temptation.

"In certain situations it's OK to break the law or rules if I'm not hurting myself or others."

#20

Most drivers think it's a bad idea to text and drive. The government agrees: every state in the continental United States, except for two, has a ban on texting while driving.[2] (A ban isn't exactly a law, but functions similarly. You can be fined up to $500 if you're caught texting and driving. In some states it results in criminal charges.) Legalities aside, breaking this rule can result in terrible tragedy. One of every four accidents in the United States is caused by a driver texting. In spite of the fact that nine people die every day from accidents caused by distractions such as texting while driving, over 30 percent of all drivers in the United States (not just teens) confess that they break this rule.[3]

This is just one example of areas where we found that Christian young women across the nation believed the lie that, "In certain situations it is OK to break the law or rules if I'm not hurting myself or others." (Even if you feel you're not hurting someone because you've broken laws and no one has gotten hurt, it doesn't mean you couldn't live with serious regret about that or some other area of disobedience in the future. Here's the thing: rules are in place because the potential to hurt yourself or others exists.) In addition to texting while driving, some girls said it was OK to illegally download music. Others felt it was OK to ignore underage drinking laws. Underlying all these deceptive activities is the lie that "I can sin and get away with it."

BREAKING
THE **RULES**

We asked teen girls to agree or disagree with the statement "It's OK to break the law or rules if I'm not hurting myself or others." Here's how they responded:

71% Agree or sometimes agree

28% Disagree

One girl put it this way:

🍎 *I know what is right, but occasionally what I feel inside just wins out. Honestly, it sometimes depends on what I think I can get away with.*

This may be the most fundamental lie Satan tells us about sin. **He makes us believe that we won't get caught;** we won't face the music, so to speak. God had said to Adam, "If you eat the fruit of this tree, you will die." The command was clear: "Don't eat." The consequences for disobedience were equally clear: "You will die."

After Satan raised a question in Eve's mind about the goodness of God in giving such a mandate and whether God in fact had the right to control her life, he proceeded to challenge the consequences. He did so with a direct frontal attack on the word of God: *"You will not . . . die,"* the Serpent said to the woman (Genesis 3:4). Three times the writer of Psalm 10 indicates that the reason people disobey God is that they believe they can get away with it (verses 6, 11, and 13).

Further, *Satan entices us with the benefits of our sin.* In the garden he suggested to Eve, "Not only can you disobey God and avoid negative consequences; there are also some definite benefits you will experience if you eat this fruit":

"For God knows that when you eat of it your eyes will be opened, and you will be like God, knowing good and evil."
(Genesis 3:5)

THINK
ABOUT IT!

We usually sin because we think we'll get some pleasure or benefit out of it. Next time you're tempted to sin, stop and think about some of the consequences of sin. Remind yourself that:

Sin steals joy (Psalm 51:12)

Sin removes confidence (1 John 3:19–21)

Sin brings guilt (Psalm 51:3)

Sin quenches God's Spirit (1 Thessalonians 5:19)

Sin brings physical damage (Psalm 38:1–11; 31:10)

Sin causes an ache in the soul (Psalm 32:3–4)

Sin breaks God's heart (Ephesians 4:30)

Sin opens the door to other sins (Isaiah 30:1)

Sin breaks fellowship with God (Isaiah 59:1–2)

Sin produces fear (Proverbs 28:1)

Sin desires to control my life (John 8:34; Romans 6:16)

In a way, Satan was right. According to Hebrews 11:25, sin does bring us pleasure for a short time. Ultimately, however, sin exacts a devastating toll. *There are no exceptions.* The Truth is that sin, when it is full grown, gives birth to death (James 1:15).

Take, for example, a twenty-year-old college student who is in the news as we write this. He's been facing the trial of his life. You see, one year ago he secured a fake ID, enabling him to drink illegally. When he took off from a party he was asked to leave for becoming violent, his blood alcohol level was .242. (The legal blood alcohol limit for driving under the influence is .08. He was way over!) At two thirty in the morning, he got behind the wheel of his car. On his way home, he struck two young men so hard it knocked one right out of his shoes. That man didn't survive. The other victim is in a wheelchair due to brain damage. The victim of his own sin, this young man faced vehicular homicide charges and was found guilty and sentenced to prison.

The consequences of sin are great. Don't mess with the rules. They are there to protect you. Even if the consequences aren't immediately visible, you can't break rules (God's or others') without ultimately hurting yourself and others.

#21 { "I can't control myself when I'm stressed or PMS-ing." }

Warning: do not read this while you are PMS-ing.

I (Dannah) was sitting in my tenth-grade lunch period when a bout of PMS proved to be nearly deadly. That is, if taking a sack lunch in the temples is at all lethal.

I hate to even confess this, but oh well! I was talking with my friends during lunch at my Christian high school. The teacher decided we were talking too loudly. I confess that I always thought of her as a killjoy and immediately had a resentful heart when she confronted us. On a regular day, that would have been the end of my sin.

Not on this day.

I guess I wasn't really that quiet.

She confronted us again. I felt that horrible sensation when your pulse rages out of control. You begin to tear up—out of either anger or emotional pain. It's hard to tell. I stuffed my lunch into its paper sack and headed for the door.

As I passed my teacher, I threw a stunning curveball (aka crushed-up lunch) at the garbage can that was right beside her desk.

I missed.

It hit her in the left temple.

Yes, I was in a world of trouble.

No, my parents didn't show any mercy.

Ever have PMS get the best of you?

Symptoms can range from mild bloating and cramping to all-out depression, extreme body fatigue, sleeplessness, headaches, anxiety, food cravings, loss of coordination, recurrent yeast or bladder infections, and, of course, the ever-lovely, supersized breakout. PMS is a very real physical malady. One young woman we spoke to had literally dropped out of school for a few months because it seemed to her that her symptoms had begun to rule her life:

We searched for months to figure out what was wrong with me. I was checked for blood disorders, urinary tract

OVERCOMING **P.M.S.**
(PRETTY MEAN STUFF!)

Cooperate with your body when you sense that you are plagued with PMS. Chart your physical and emotional symptoms for a few months and learn when you are most vulnerable to sin. (Yep, we just called it sin.) Then, try these things for starters:

➡ **Reduce Stress**—Don't take the SATs during your worst time of the month, if you can help it. Try scheduling fewer appointments and cutting back on obligations. Leave extra time for devos and bubble baths during your hardest week.

➡ **Get Physical**—Regular exercise has a profound effect on brain function and health. Find something you love like tennis, Pilates, or walking your pooch and be consistent all month long. You'll see an improvement.

➡ **Eat Well**—If you can eliminate the blood-sugar peaks and valleys that soda, sweets, and carbs create, you'll have fewer mood swings. If you focus on green veggies and lots of water during the worst time of your month (the time that you want to scarf down bag after bag of Doritos), you'll feel better.

➡ **Post a Scripture verse to pray for control**—We recommend Psalm 19:14, which we've printed on the next page for you.

If you're still struggling, get a complete physical checkup; ask a physician if there are any physical issues that need to be treated medically.

infections, neurological problems. Nothing panned out. I just knew I was exhausted, in pain most of the month, and nasty as can be to my friends and, especially, my mom. Turns out it was just PMS.

However real they may be, physical symptoms of any kind are never an excuse for sin. Just as being tired cannot be an excuse for hatred, unkindness, emotional outbursts, or physical aggression, neither can PMS be. You don't have to be controlled by your hormones.

Maybe you struggle with self-control at other times of the month, when you're just feeling stressed. Do you ever feel justified in consuming crazy amounts of junk food, skipping out on responsibilities, or lashing out at your parents when your stress levels go up?

EAT CHOCOLATE!
Yes, we know you want it. Turns out, it is actually good for you during "that time of the month." Darker is better.

At its root, anxiety is a belief issue. It's about more than what's needed to release the pressure valve. When stress makes us act out of control, we're telling God, "I can't cast my cares on You and expect You to actually take care of this." It's a condition of the heart that gives way to many other sins—things like anger, fear, worry, and sleeplessness from obsession. Whether it's hormones or homework that place your feet on a downward spiral, the answer is found in God's Truth.

You can choose to focus on Christ and bring every thought and word obedient to Him. God's Word encourages us to *"take every thought captive to obey Christ"* (2 Corinthians 10:5).

When you focus on Jesus and His Word, you will be able to bring your emotions under His control. Here's a good verse to post on your bedroom wall, your bathroom mirror, or the dash of your car:

> ## "LET THE WORDS OF MY MOUTH AND THE MEDITATION OF MY HEART BE ACCEPTABLE IN YOUR SIGHT, O LORD, MY ROCK AND MY REDEEMER." (PSALM 19:14)

Every word and every thought is examined by God. Even those we have and speak during that emotionally wealthy time of the month or a super stressful time like finals week. By God's grace, you can choose how you respond and how your emotions are expressed.

the lie

the truth

I can't overcome my sin.

• You are powerless to change yourself. John 15:5

• Any person who is born again has a new nature and has the power of Christ to overcome sin. Romans 6:6–7

• Every child of God has been given the body of Christ to help overcome sin. James 5:16; Galatians 5:1

In certain situations it's OK to break the law or rules if I'm not hurting myself or others.

• Satan entices us with the "benefits" of sin. Genesis 3:4; Hebrews 11:25

• We may not experience the consequences of our sin right away, but there will be consequences. James 1:15; Galatians 6:7

I can't control myself when I'm stressed or PMS-ing.

• What happens in our bodies is real, but physical symptoms can never be an excuse for sin. James 4:17; 2 Corinthians 12:9–10

• By God's grace you can bring your emotions, thoughts, and words captive to Jesus Christ. 2 Corinthians 10:5b

• God examines every word we speak and every thought that we think. Psalms 139:23; 94:11; Matthew 9:4

making it personal

Don't feel condemned. There is no condemnation if you are in Christ Jesus. But lean into the conviction! How? By journaling some Truth, of course. Focus on answering these questions as you write:

What lies have I been most likely to believe about sin?

What Scripture verses can I store in my heart to help me counter those lies with the Truth?

Mandi

Hey friend! Got a minute?

Sure! What's up?!?!

Need some advice . . . I usually put on music to stop thinking . . . to chill out and relax. I don't really pay attention to the words. Once I really look at it and I start thinking about what they're saying, I realize it's not what I want to be listening to but it's already in my head. I think this might be affecting me. Thoughts?

I hear ya! Some days I make time to be with God, but other days I end up listening to music for a lot longer than I thought I would . . . that takes time away from God. So . . . I think it is affecting you . . . and ME!

Let's make a plan to get into God's Word. Throne before the phone.

DEAL!!!

"Movies can and do
have tremendous power
in shaping young lives."

WALT DISNEY

Lies about Media

Two hundred years ago, what sounds could you have heard?

You could have heard things like human voices . . . nature sounds . . . musical instruments. You could *not* have heard sounds that were electronically produced. No radios, no TVs, no DVD players, no laptops, no music streaming, no game systems . . .

For the first several thousand years of history, humans were not bombarded with artificial or electronic stimuli. Further, they had relatively little information coming at them. All that has changed in this high-tech era when we live with an explosion of information and acute sensory overload.

Technology today provides an amazing array of options that your parents and grandparents could not have imagined when they were teens. It has dramatically changed the way we communicate and relate to other people and has made it possible for us to be endlessly entertained with games, movies, TV shows, music, memes, etc.

Many of you go to bed with your ear buds in your ears and wake up with them still there. After a quick shower, you plug them back in for the commute to school. During that commute, you may check your text messages or make a quick call on your cell. During the school day, you'll likely take every legal opportunity—and perhaps a few illegal opportunities—to check those text messages or see if you've received any new Instagram likes. (One study out of UCLA revealed that we crave those "likes" because our brain gets a jolt of dopamine, a "feel good" chemical, when we hear the sound associated with them or see the numbers go up!)[1]

At home, you settle in to binge-watch your favorite show or a few hours of really deep conversation via Snapchat. (Read with sarcasm.)

Recently, God assigned a handful of college-aged women to me (Dannah) to disciple. I started my relationship with them by asking for two nights and three days to sequester them from the craze of the world and hide themselves in God's presence and His Word. We drove up, up, up into the mountains to a delightful little wood cabin by a lake. We would have campfires, make s'mores, take rides in a canoe, sit in the shade, and take hikes during our three days of seeking God. I thought the girls would be thrilled with the care and attention I'd taken to find a special place for them, but two of them actually went into hysterics when they found out they would not have cell service. One of the girls cried for an hour. (Can you say addicted?)

No other generation has had so much technology at their disposal, and you love it. You don't hang out at the soda parlor like your great-grandparents did. You hang out in cyberspace. We don't believe that technology—whether used for social networking or entertainment—is inherently "bad"; it has its benefits. We do believe that using it mindlessly is a huge danger zone. We want to make sure that you're controlling it and it's not controlling you.

Our conversations with young women revealed that this is an area where many of them are particularly resistant to change. You may be tempted to "tune us out" on this one. We would appeal to you to put all your media on "pause" for a few moments, open your heart, and consider whether you may be believing any lies in relation to your media use. For example:

#22 { "The benefits of constant media use outweigh the harm." }

This was one of the most universally believed lies. Almost every young woman we spoke to (98 percent!) agreed that their media habits negatively affect their relationship with God and others. But they believed the benefits were worth it. What kind of benefits?

 Social media connects me to my friends.

 I usually put on music when I want to quit thinking.

 The Internet is like reading. I think when I'm on there.

 I'll see a pretty girl on YouTube, and she'll be dressed a certain way, and I know that's what's in style. So it pretty much keeps me in fashion.

Need we go on? The girls themselves admitted that some of the benefits were pretty shallow, yet they could not seem to change their media habits. Let's see if we can motivate you.

[lies young women believe]

First, *keep in mind that Hollywood recognizes the power of media and that many of the artists who make movies and music feel the need to filter it for their own kids.*

One controversial rap singer admits that he cuts a family-friendly version of his songs for just his daughter because he doesn't want her exposed to the violence, sex, and cussing. The stuff many of you expose yourselves to is content that those making the filth won't even expose their own families to.

Second, *realize that your media habits do change you.* Ask anyone who went out to buy Reese's Pieces after watching *E.T.,* in which a cute little alien ate the then little known candy. The candy's sales increased by 65 percent when the movie was released. (Talking about them kind of makes you want some right now, doesn't it?) There are often strong behavioral

We first asked young women to respond to the statement **"The media has no effect on me."** No one agreed, yet there was a resistance to filter media choices. So, we asked them to respond to this statement: **"The media has a negative influence on my relationship with God and others, but its benefits are worth it."** Here's what they said:

98% Agree or sometimes agree

2% Disagree

changes in audiences like the little girl who flushed her goldfish down the toilet bowl to free it after watching *Finding Nemo.*[2] You might think that's funny (though not for the goldfish), but it wasn't funny when two teenagers died and dozens were injured mirroring the death-defying challenge to lie on a busy highway after watching a football movie titled *The Program.*[3]

If you think you are immune to behavior changes influenced by your media choices, think again. Horror novelist Stephen King once said, "Movies are the highest popular art of our time, and art has the ability to change lives."[4] We are not immune from buying what they want us to buy, dressing how they want us to dress, and valuing what they want us to value. Most of the girls we talked to recognized this risk. Two of them said:

🍎 *You're sitting there watching this box from an outsider's point of view. You might watch it for an hour. Then for two hours. You watch this box! You might not make all of the connections right then, but you'll see a pretty girl, and she will be getting all this attention, and you eventually think if you are pretty like she is, you'll get attention.*

I don't really pay attention to the words of music. Once I really start looking at it and start thinking about what they are saying, I realize that it is not what I want to be listening to. But it's too late. It's already in my head.

If you are taking in regular or significant doses of music, television, the Internet, and movies, you are being affected by them. The question is: Are you being influenced positively or negatively? The impact is usually not felt immediately—it's more like an IV in your arm that goes *drip . . . drip . . . drip . . .* gradually pumping a foreign substance into your system. If the substance dripping through that plastic tubing is toxic or poisonous, you may not feel the results right away, but once it gets into your system, your whole body will definitely be affected!

Likewise, the consequences of taking toxic media into your mind and soul may not be realized until further down the road when it's too late and the damage has been done.

It all comes down to whether you're going to let the world's values, morals, and thinking drip day by day into your system, or you're going to intentionally choose to be exposed to input that will help you become more wise and godly. If you're ready to take positive action in your entertainment media choices, here are some simple steps for starters:

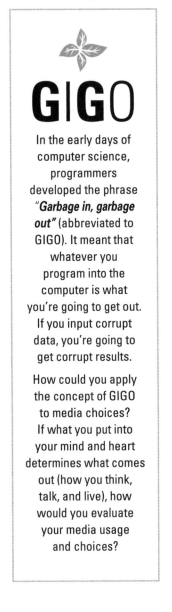

GIGO

In the early days of computer science, programmers developed the phrase *"Garbage in, garbage out"* (abbreviated to GIGO). It meant that whatever you program into the computer is what you're going to get out. If you input corrupt data, you're going to get corrupt results.

How could you apply the concept of GIGO to media choices? If what you put into your mind and heart determines what comes out (how you think, talk, and live), how would you evaluate your media usage and choices?

PREVIEW YOUR CHOICES. Check out
your movies, television series, magazines, songs, or websites. Get an opinion from a trustworthy source. Your parents and youth pastor are a great place to begin. You can also use Internet services like PluggedIn.com that provide free reviews of movies, television programs, and music. Getting a mature, godly perspective is wise; it will help guard your heart and mind from ungodly influences and hold you accountable.

PROCESS THEM WITH A LIST OF PROS AND CONS. Having

previewed them, now write a list of pros and cons. What benefits does this media choice bring to your life? What cons does it present, especially in light of your spiritual life?

PRAY ABOUT IT. Ask the Lord to guide you in making decisions about

your media favorites that honor Him rather than indulging your desires for popularity, beauty, entertainment, and socialization.

If you don't make your decisions based on an intentional filtering system, you'll end up following the crowd—watching, listening, and communicating like everyone else. But remember—you are not just everyone else. You are God's set-apart masterpiece, and He wants you to stay pure and empty for Him to fill.

#23

A lot of the girls we spoke to estimated that they spend twenty-five to thirty-five hours per week online, text messaging, or watching Netflix. We found it interesting that girls who were homeschooled were likely to have the highest number of hours. Many felt that this was absolutely fine. Here were some of their arguments:

 Parents are just not used to it. I hate it when they get mad and they're like "get off now!" It's how my generation communicates.

 It's how I stay connected to my friends.

🍎 *Research proves that you can learn a lot of hand-eye coordination from computer games.*

As far as we know, no great athletic careers have ever been built on the hand-eye coordination learned from computer games, and great relationships are not built solely by texting. We agree that there are some great uses of the media, and your generation is comfortable with them. However, everything should have limits.

One social science project observed the behavior of children with and without limits. For the first portion of the study, children were observed during recess at a school that had a huge fence limiting where they could play. For the second portion of the study, children were observed during recess at another school where there was no fence, but an open field that enabled them to have no restrictions on where they played.

Guess who cooperated more during play and had fewer playground fights? Guess who was least likely to be fearful and teary during recess?[5]

You guessed it! The children who played behind the protective limitation of a fence were far happier during recess and even exhibited a better behavior in the classroom after recess!

Limits give us a sense of safety and, oddly, are a vital part of our freedom. More and more research is proving that computers have the deadly potential to be addictive. That is—to put you into bondage. Proverbs 25:16 says, "If you find honey, eat just enough" (NIV). In other words, show restraint. Maybe you'd get it better if it said, "If you find chocolate, eat just enough." Have you ever overeaten to the point of making yourself sick? Too much of even a good thing isn't always a good thing!

We need limits for every area of our lives, including our media habits, or we risk being harmed or getting "sick" in our souls and our relationships. Those boundaries need to be established based on the principles of God's Word and His best for you.

I (Nancy) often find myself spending way more time on electronic and social media than is wise or healthy. I could be on my iPhone just about every waking moment—texting, checking email, watching news, scrolling social media feeds, playing Words with Friends, following the Chicago Cubs (marrying a lifelong Cubs fan has changed my life in more ways than one!), and more.

There is a **RICHNESS** OF **SOUL** that cannot be cultivated without regular seasons of quiet and solitude.

My phone can be a great tool for staying connected with friends and keeping up on what's happening in the world. But the truth is, I often end up wasting valuable time and energy that could be used more productively. In the process, my heart and hunger for the Lord and His Word suffer and I can end up isolating myself from face-to-face relationships with people.

Tons of research has been done about how our phones and social media are changing our lives and rewiring our minds—mostly not for the better. Knowing how addictive these things are in my own life, I've found it important to establish practical limits for using my iPhone.

(My husband has helped me with this. I'd encourage you to let a good friend or your parents help hold you accountable.) Hard as it is for me to exercise self-control in this area, those limits have proved to be a great blessing—they help me guard my heart from spiritual "intruders," cultivate greater passion for Christ, and be more "present" with others.

Here's one more thing we want you to think about. We've noticed that people who spend most of their waking hours plugged in to media have a hard time getting still enough and quiet enough long enough to think or to let God speak to them through His Word.

There is a richness of soul that cannot be cultivated without regular seasons of quiet and solitude. There is a depth in our relationships with God and others that cannot be experienced apart from times of unhurried, face-to-face conversation.

God may not direct you to establish exactly the same boundaries as we have or as another friend has. But we want to urge you not to just "go with the flow" when it comes to your media usage. Be intentional about setting limits on what you'll expose yourself to and how much time you'll spend online, on your computer, or text messaging each day or week.

MEDIA MANIA

Not sure if you should ditch the media in your life or make it the main event? Maybe for you, it's just a matter of setting better limits. Use these simple questions to guide you.

➡ **Does it** violate the standard of Philippians 4:8? *("Whatever is true, whatever is honorable, whatever is just, whatever is pure, whatever is lovely, whatever is commendable, if there is any excellence, if there is anything worthy of praise, think about these things.")*

➡ **Would you** be embarrassed to watch it with Jesus?

➡ **Does it** create conflict between you and your parents?

➡ **Is it** something you have to hide?

➡ **Does it** cause you to isolate yourself from family members or friends?

➡ **Does it** cause you to neglect other responsibilities?

➡ **Do you** have a greater appetite for media, social networking, or entertainment than you do for spending time in God's Word or in other activities that nourish your spiritual life?

➡ **Are you** addicted? (Here's a great way to find out if you're addicted to a particular form of media: give it up for 30 days. If you can't do it, you're addicted!)

If you answered yes to any of the above, ask the Lord to help you evaluate your media usage and establish wise boundaries that are pleasing to Him and healthy for you!

DOUSING LIES WITH THE TRUTH

the lie

The benefits of constant media use outweigh the harm.

It's not a waste of time . . . even if it is, it's OK.

the truth

• Media exerts a powerful influence on us. What you look at and listen to will change you—for better or worse. Luke 11:34

• We are called to make wise media choices. Philippians 4:8

• Every area of our life needs boundaries. Philippians 4:5; Ephesians 5:15–17

• Boundaries give us freedom and protection. Proverbs 25:16; Galatians 5:13

• We need to be intentional about our media choices. Psalm 101:3–4

[lies young women believe]

making it personal

THERE'S REALLY NO PRECEDENT FOR HOW TO RESPOND TO THIS MEDIA-DRIVEN SOCIETY.

You and your friends will need to lead the way in Truth. Why not begin by busting down some lies in your own life through some "journal therapy"? As you write, focus on answering these simple questions:

What lies have I been most likely to believe about media?

What Scripture verses can I store in my heart to help me counter those lies with the Truth?

Lish

My mother!! She is always telling me how she wants me to marry the "perfect" guy and raise a bunch of kids and have the American dream. #whatever

Annoying!

I am just not sure I want that! I am a very pro-independent woman! That is VERY much what I am about.

You are so right!! It's not about families and having kids anymore. Women are supposed to have careers too! But the Bible stresses marriage and families so maybe there is something there. IDK.

For me the whole family thing is overrated!

You got me thinking . . . I'm going to look into it. I think it could be cool. I kinda wish there wasn't so much pressure NOT to want a family.

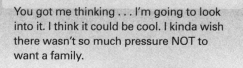

"Resolved, never,
henceforward, till I die,
to act as if I were any way
my own, but entirely
and altogether God's."

JONATHAN EDWARDS

12

Lies about the Future

Satan has been attacking femininity since he first tempted Eve. He has done so with increased ferocity over the past seventy years or so, since the feminist revolution swept through our culture in the mid-1900s.

The mantra of this movement was "women can do anything men can do." Convinced that women needed the same jobs and pay as men, women like Gloria Steinem led the way to redefining *woman*. They burned a few bras here and signed a few petitions there and won the attention of women and men alike.

Today women can hold the same jobs as men, but there is little in our culture today that encourages those women to make being a wife and a mother a priority. In their quest for equality, feminists have undermined the concepts of motherhood and homemaking.

Our culture has been profoundly changed as a result, and countless lives and homes have been scarred and broken.

Nowhere is this revolution seen more obviously than in our view of marriage and career. Those things may not be an issue for you anytime soon; however, we'd like to talk to you about them right now if you can curl up for some serious girl talk!

#24 { "Having a career outside the home is more valuable and fulfilling than being 'just' a wife and mom." }

🍎 *For me the whole family idea is kind of overrated.*

🍎 *It is not about families and having kids anymore. Women are expected to have careers, too.*

🍎 *It has become uncool to want a husband and a family.*

Sadly, most women are clueless as to what God has to say about these things. For more than fifty years, our whole culture has been brainwashed with a concept of what it means to be female that is contrary to God's Word. (Since He's the One who made men and women, He's the One who decides how they're supposed to function!) Your generation hasn't had a lot of role models of women who function according to God's design.

As a result, many women are offended at the thought that there are any differences between men and women (except for the obvious physiological ones). Concepts like femininity, submission, or respecting men are foreign to them. Many women even hate men (some in response to men who have treated them in ways that are contrary to godly masculinity).

As a younger woman, I (Nancy) was not directly influenced by the feminist philosophy. However, I was tempted with a variation that was equally deceptive. As a teenager, I had a strong desire to serve the Lord. Somehow I developed the mindset that if I'd been a man, God could have used my life in a more significant way. I struggled to understand and accept God's unique calling for me as a woman.

When I was in my twenties, I began to search God's Word to discover why God designed men and

FUELING
YOUR PASSION!

Here are some ideas for fueling a passion for being a mom and wife. Try one today!

Pull a random act of kindness by surprise babysitting. You won't believe how much it'll knock that young mom's socks off if you show up with a babysitting kit in hand to love on her kids.

"Ding-dong ditch" a batch of freshly baked cookies. Think of someone who is discouraged—a neighbor or family you know. Make them some fresh cookies. Deliver them to their front door and run!

Write a letter to God. Tell Him about your fears of motherhood or marriage. Write out your hopes and dreams. He wants to hear it all!

Make a school assignment a project in defending marriage or motherhood. Have a paper or speech due soon? Why not delve into the subject of God's design for women?

women differently and why He assigned them distinct roles. Over the next several years, the Lord opened my eyes to the beauty of His amazing design and plan. I became truly grateful for the privilege of being a woman and excited about the opportunity to fulfill His calling for my life.

Let's take a look at what He says.

In Genesis 2:18 we find an important insight into why God created the first woman:

> "THEN THE LORD GOD SAID, 'IT IS NOT GOOD
> THAT THE MAN SHOULD BE ALONE;
> I WILL MAKE HIM A HELPER FIT FOR HIM.'"

There you have it—**God created Eve to be a helper to Adam**—to complete him, to be suited to his needs. ("Hold it," you may be saying. "Now I'm completely turned off." Stick with us!) The woman was made from the man, made for the man, and given as God's gift to the man. Together with her husband, they were to love and serve the Lord who made them for His glory.

While God sets apart some women to serve Him as singles, marriage (between one man and one woman) is His design for most. And if that is His plan for you, there is no more fulfilling or significant calling you could have.

There's another good reason God created us as women. He wants husbands and wives to fulfill what He commanded them to do in Genesis 1:28. God's first command to them was: *"Be fruitful and multiply and fill the earth and subdue it."*

Together, the man and his wife were to fill the earth by having children, who in turn would have other children. The woman was uniquely designed and equipped to be a bearer and nurturer of life. In fact, Eve's name means "life."

Sadly, these two roles—wife and mother—have come under attack in our culture. The result is that even the church isn't committed to protecting them. In 1987, only 20 percent of Christians felt that women should *not* emphasize these two roles. In 2007, just twenty years later, this had grown to 47 percent who felt that the roles of marriage and motherhood should *not* be emphasized for women.[1] That survey was over a decade ago. Our experience suggests that this trend has continued to grow.

A lot of young women today fear marriage (perhaps because they've not seen a lot of great examples). And increasingly, young married women are choosing not to have children or to delay motherhood until they've had a chance to do everything else they want to do in life.

Who will protect these vital roles? We hope you will. We hope you can see that they are worth protecting. Now, we realize that your feathers may be a bit ruffled right now. Given the way we're programmed by the world, God's Truth is a stark contrast. So, let's see if we can soften it up a bit by getting a unique perspective.

I (Dannah) sat down with my son, Rob, and his best friend, Ryan, to get a guy's perspective on all this. What these two godly guys had to say was compelling.

Dannah: What do you guys think makes a woman a woman?

(Nervous laughter followed by dumbfounded silence!)

Dannah: OK, let's try another approach. Do you think it is OK for a woman to want to be a wife and mother?

Rob and Ryan in unison: Yes! Definitely!

FOOD FOR THOUGHT ON BEING
GOD'S GIRL!

If you want to fuel your passion for biblical womanhood, check out these blogs (after you visit **LiesYoungWomenBelieve.com**, of course!):

GirlTalkHome.com
GirlDefined.com

Dannah: Do you think girls in your generation feel the freedom to want that?

Rob and Ryan in unison: No. Not at all.

Ryan: It's so wrong, because girls feel pressure *not* to be a wife and mother. It's not like they feel pressure to be a career woman. It's a negative thing. It's bad. Society puts this pressure on them.

Rob: It's not like she *can* have a career. It's like she *should* have one.

Dannah: Do you think that's fair?

Rob: Not at all. If a guy had that attitude about not wanting a wife and kids, he'd be considered a jerk. I don't get it. Just like we're supposed to want to protect a wife and be a great dad, girls should want to have a husband and be a great mom.

Eureka! That's it, isn't it? If there were a men's movement to absolve them of their right to be a great husband and dad, it would quickly be shot down. No woman would want to marry a man who said, "Babe, you're cool and everything, but I'm not that into the family thing. The most important thing in my life is going to be my career. If you want to hang out while I pursue it, whatever!" No way! We want someone who is hook, line, and sinker in love with us and wants to make our relationship the most important earthly love they ever pursue.

In my conversation with Rob and Ryan, Ryan said, "The world is telling girls that they don't have the freedom to even choose to pursue being a wife and a mom."

We are telling you that you do! You do have the freedom to choose to live out God's designed role for you and the adventure, romance, love, and blessings that come with it.

Not only do you have the *freedom* to fully embrace God's design for women—not only is it an incredible *privilege*—but as a child of God, you have a *responsibility* to fulfill His calling and His purpose for your life as a woman. And for most women that means embracing marriage and motherhood as a vital and God-given mission and calling.

Still a little miffed at all of this? Relax! We want you to understand that we're not saying you won't do other amazing things. The Proverbs 31 pattern of woman demonstrates first a woman who is an excellent wife and mother. But she's also a manufacturer, importer, manager, realtor, farmer, seamstress, upholsterer, and merchant! She is strong and successful in many areas of her life. However, she doesn't neglect her relationship with God or her calling as a wife and mother. Her sense of fulfillment and value doesn't come from her achievements, impressive as they are. It comes from being submitted to God's plan for her life. Her reverence for God opens her up to a great adventure.

Want the great adventure?

We've found it in embracing God's plan for womanhood.

We believe you will too.

#25 { "What I do now doesn't affect the future." }

As we were writing this, a young female celebrity who was once a sweet-faced child star was in trouble (again) for being drunk. Magazines displayed photos of her passed out in a car after a night of hard partying. Her fans quickly came to her defense. One wrote:

🍎 *People really need to ease up on the girl. If every twenty-year-old were thrown into rehab for drinking and partying, the colleges would be empty. It's a rite of passage for many people. [She] will be just fine.*[2]

That mentality pervades our culture. It says, "What you do now doesn't affect the future." Believing this lie feeds so many others. A great example of this is how so many we spoke to say they intended to marry a Christian, but since they weren't looking for a marriage partner yet, they could go out with non-Christians. This thinking is so dangerous.

What you choose to do now will either form habits you have to break in the future or habits that are helpful to you. Galatians 6:7 says, "Do not be deceived: God is not mocked, for whatever one sows, that will he also reap." If you plant corn, you're not going to soon have turnips tumbling out of your garden. In the same way, every action has results. If you plant to please your own desires, you'll reap a crop of consequences. If you plant to please God, you'll reap joy, peace, and everlasting life.

> ## "YOU ARE WHAT YOU HAVE BEEN BECOMING."
> Art DeMoss
> *As spoken to Nancy as a child*

Habits are a result of seemingly insignificant individual choices and acts that you sow when you're twelve, fifteen, or twenty. They can be good or bad. You'll reap what you sow. You're sowing seeds now. What you do with your time, your eating habits, your exercise habits, the way you talk to your parents, the way you treat your friends, the way you spend your money, the way you work, your sleep habits . . . These are habits you are developing today.

I (Nancy) made a lot of unwise choices about what to eat when I was a teenager and in my twenties. I ate more meals than you can imagine at a fast-food chain that shall remain unnamed—actually I would order a hamburger (make that a double burger with cheese, ketchup, and pickles) and fries at the drive-through and inhale them in my car on my way to wherever I was headed next. To this day, it has been a major challenge in my life to develop healthy eating habits.

➡ CHOICES MATTER:

the **books** you read

the **magazines** you read

the **television** programs you watch

the **music** you listen to

the **conversations** you have

the **friends** you choose

what time you **go to bed**

what time you **get up in the morning**

Little things matter a lot.

There's one habit that was emphasized more than any other in my (Nancy's) home as I was growing up. *I don't think there is any more important habit you could possibly develop as a teen. It's the practice of spending consistent time getting to know God through His Word.* Every aspect of your life, short term and long term, will be affected by this one habit.

I am so grateful that my parents modeled this practice and encouraged me to develop a consistent devotional life as a young girl. I cannot adequately express what a huge difference this habit has made in my life.

I'm not saying it's easy—as much as I value my time with the Lord, there have been plenty of mornings when I've allowed the pillow, my laptop, or other distractions to win out and ended up spending only a few hurried moments with Him. But I know that I can't be the woman God made me to be apart from having an intimate relationship with Him. And that requires spending time on a regular basis listening to Him speak through His Word and responding to Him in worship and prayer.

Over the years, I have challenged women to get started in this area by making a commitment to *spend at least some time with the Lord in His Word every day for the next thirty days.* Thousands of women have taken that challenge, and many have written back and told me what a difference it has made in their lives. Would you be willing to take that same "thirty-day challenge"? I can't think of a single habit that will have a greater impact on your life over the long haul.

 THE THIRTY-DAY CHALLENGE

I commit to spend time with the Lord in His Word every day for the next thirty days.

Signed _____

Date _____

Once you start to experience the blessings of meditating on God's Word and spending time alone in His presence, we believe this is a habit you will want to maintain for the rest of your life!

DOUSING LIES WITH THE TRUTH

the lie

the truth

Having a career outside the home is more valuable and fulfilling than being "just" a wife and mom.

• There is nothing more valuable or fulfilling than doing what God has made and called you to do.
Isaiah 43:7; 1 Corinthians 10:31

• For most women, an important part of their God-given calling is to glorify God through marriage.
Genesis 2:18; Titus 2:3–4

• Motherhood is another vital calling in God's kingdom.
Genesis 1:28; Titus 2:4

• God may give you different assignments at different seasons of your life. You will not have to violate one priority to fulfill another.
Proverbs 31:10–31

What I do now doesn't affect the future.

• Your choices today have consequences and are forming habits—good or bad—that you will take into your future.
Galatians 6:7

• The most important habit you can form is cultivating a relationship with God in His Word and prayer.
Psalms 1:2–3; 119:97

[lies young women believe]

making it personal

WHAT LIES HAVE YOU BELIEVED ABOUT YOUR FUTURE?

Why not turn them over to the Lord so He can truly direct and protect your life? Grab that journal once more and answer these questions:

What lies have I been most likely to believe about my future?

What Scripture verses can I store in my heart to help me counter those lies with the Truth?

Overcoming Lies

"Make no provision for the
flesh, to gratify its desires."

ROMANS 13:14

13

How to Stop Fueling the Lies

Stop **listening to** and **dwelling** on them

My (Nancy's) house was once besieged with fruit flies. It all started when some friends asked if they could make grape juice in my kitchen (we're talking 150 quarts of grape juice!). The bushels of freshly picked grapes and all the large pots filled with grapes in the juicing process drew a swarm of the pesky insects that eventually made their way upstairs to my study as I was working on this book.

My friends knew just the solution: They put a small piece of banana in the bottom of a drinking glass. (Fruit flies love fruit!) Then they made a paper cone, cut a tiny hole in the tip, placed the cone in the glass with the tip pointed down, and taped the top of the cone securely to the rim of the glass. I set the contraption on a shelf next to my desk, where I waited and watched as I continued working.

What happened over the next several hours was a vivid illustration of what we've been talking about in this book—the way humans end up in bondage to sin—"trapped"! One after another, dozens of those tiny little flies were attracted to the glass by the scent of the banana. One after another, they descended into the paper cone, through the hole, and into the glass. And one after another, they found themselves trapped,

THE **APOSTLE PAUL'S** **ADVICE** ON LISTENING AND DWELLING

The apostle Paul urges us to think about "whatever is true, whatever is honorable, whatever is just, whatever is pure, whatever is lovely, whatever is commendable" (Philippians 4:8). If we listen to messages that encourage us to be pure, noble, righteous, lovely, and admirable, we'll become like that. And if we listen to input that is impure and deceptive, we'll likely take on those characteristics.

unable to escape. They got in, lured by the banana. Once they were in, they couldn't get out.

I was reminded of James 1, which describes how temptation works in our lives:

Each person is tempted when he is lured and enticed by his own desire *[just as those fruit flies are lured and enticed when they smell that banana!]*. Then desire when it has conceived gives birth to sin *[they fly into the trap]*, and sin when it is fully grown brings forth death. (James 1:14–15)

As I watched those flies make their way into the glass that proved to be a deadly trap, I thought of Eve—eyeing that luscious fruit, thinking how much pleasure it would bring her, and finally going for the lure—only to find that the thing she thought would fulfill her actually paved the way to her coffin.

Then I thought of myself and how often I have "gone for the lure" and ended up enslaved to the very things I thought would make me happy.

You've probably got this into your head by now, but let's review two basic facts upon which this book has been built. First:

BELIEVING A LIE PLACES US IN BONDAGE.

In our first few chapters, we outlined the progression of how lies lead to bondage:

We LISTEN to a lie. ⟶ **We get too close.**

We DWELL on the lie. ⟶ **We focus on it and ponder the benefits.**

We BELIEVE the lie. ⟶ **We begin to believe the lie is true.**

We ACT on the lie. ⟶ **We sin.**

As we make sinful choices based on the lies we've believed, we find that the Enemy has set a deadly trap for us—and we end up in bondage. Truly, a girl is a slave "to whatever has mastered" her (2 Peter 2:19 NIV). You may have begun to recognize this progression in your own life.

Throughout this book, we've tried to expose the Deceiver and some of the lies you may have fallen for. That's an important part of overcoming lies. But we have an even more important goal, which brings us to the second key fact upon which this book was built. We want you to know that, no matter how trapped in your bondage you may feel:

THE TRUTH HAS THE POWER TO SET US FREE.

Freedom! That's what we want for you. We're not talking about being free to do anything you want to do. True freedom is the power to do what God wants you to do; it is being free from the control of sinful ways of thinking, sinful attitudes, and sinful behavior patterns. It's knowing that by God's grace, you can say no to sin and yes to God. Instead of being in bondage to the consequences of believing lies, you can be free.

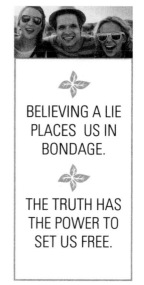

BELIEVING A LIE PLACES US IN BONDAGE.

THE TRUTH HAS THE POWER TO SET US FREE.

FREE	to accept the beauty God chose to express when He made you.
FREE	to enjoy the food He created.
FREE	to wait for God's perfect timing to find the right guy.
FREE	to be more concerned about being a friend than having one.
FREE	to be kind and gracious, even during "that time of the month"!
FREE	from the hurts of the past so you can embrace your future.
FREE	to be the same person no matter who is around.

Does that sound like something you'd like to experience?

In this final section of the book, we want to show you how you can live in that kind of freedom.

For starters, if you're going to overcome the lies that have put you in bondage, you've got to stop fueling those lies. That means being intentional about not listening to or dwelling on input that is contrary to God's Truth.

STOP LISTENING TO THE LIE

I (Dannah) was channel surfing with my daughter Lexi one day when we came upon *My Super Sweet Sixteen*. Maybe you've seen it. The "reality" TV show follows spoiled fifteen-year-old girls as they plan their sixteenth birthday party with a price tag anywhere in the range of $10,000 to

$500,000. One girl planned an all-pink party complete with pink poodles, pink food, and a pink cake. All she needed was a pink car. (Oh, wait! She already had TWO!)

Intrigued at the obvious ignorance of it all, Lexi and I watched.

"What do you think about that?" I asked Lexi at a commercial break.

"I think this is completely stupid," she answered, much to my delight.

"Do you think it's OK to watch it?" I asked.

"It's OK," she said tentatively. "It's obvious how spoiled they are, and no one would want to be like that. I'd just be afraid that if I watched it a lot, I *would* start to be like that."

BINGO!

Exposing yourself to lies, no matter how seemingly innocent, is the first step to believing them. Rule number one to overcoming lies: *Stop listening to them.*

Examine what you are putting into your mind through television, movies, the Internet, music, and even conversations with friends. You may think that it won't hurt to be exposed to ungodly ways of thinking in those mediums, but you might not realize how subtly those deceptive philosophies can influence your thinking. That's why God promises a special blessing to anyone who "walks not in the counsel of the wicked, nor stands in the way of sinners, nor sits in the seat of scoffers" (Psalm 1:1).

(If the lies you're most concerned about are ones you didn't choose to expose yourself to—like a parent telling you that you're stupid or a grandmother insisting that your newfound faith is nothing but a temporary "crutch"—you can't necessarily stop the exposure, but you *can* stop the progression. Stick with us!)

STOP DWELLING ON THE LIE

If listening is the first step in exposure, dwelling is the next. Listening is a passing notice—often just a curious exposure. Dwelling is an intentional, focused gaze. It's letting that lie move in to live with you—whether literally or figuratively.

Melissa Moore, daughter of Bible teacher Beth Moore, knows something about dwelling on a lie. During her junior year of high school, Melissa became infatuated with the fashion industry and became obsessed with fashion, fashion magazines, and body size. As she read those fashion magazines, she fell for the lie that beauty was defined by how much you weighed . . . or, rather, how much you *didn't* weigh. She listened to the lie.

[lies young women believe]

Then, she began to dwell on it. She covered her bedroom wall with cutouts from the magazines. She recalls:

🍎 *The walls were filled with pictures of women that resembled skeletons. I tacked these on my walls to remind myself that I was forbidden to eat and that I was fat. I would not pass the pictures without a deep feeling of worthlessness and shame.*[1]

The more she dwelled on these and other lies, the more she began to believe them and then to act on them. She plunged headfirst into an extended period of not eating until she was "deathly skinny, popular, and completely miserable."

It's not hard to see how we dwell on lies. Maybe *you've* posted pictures of skeletal models on the walls of your bedrooms. Maybe the pictures you post aren't of girls you compare yourself to, but guys you lust after. Maybe you regularly visit websites that teach you how to cut or binge. Maybe you load your locker with junk food and live for the bell to ring so you can hit McD's.

If you want to break free from the bondage of those lies, you've got to stop pouring fuel on them—you've got to stop dwelling on them. That will likely require making a change in your daily life. Maybe for a time you can't go shopping to overcome your appetite for buying things you don't need and can't afford (and ending up in the bondage of credit card debt). Maybe you need to get rid of your phone for a few weeks to stop obsessing about your text messages.

When Melissa finally realized what those magazine cutouts were doing to her spirit, she and her mom took drastic action—they ripped the pictures off the walls. Through much prayer, counsel, and discipline, she was able to gain some weight and put an end to an eating disorder that had gotten out of control.

Are you in bondage to a sinful habit or attitude that's being fueled by listening to and dwelling on lies?

As long as you fight the surface issues, you'll never win. Your real problem is not self-loathing, having sex with your boyfriend, or lying—any more than Eve's problem was a piece of fruit! There are underlying lies you've believed that have made you vulnerable to these forms of bondage. If you want freedom, you've got to identify what those lies are and eliminate anything that has been pouring fuel on those lies!

Do you see how it works?

OK, let's put it into practice in your life right now.

MOVING FROM BONDAGE TO FREEDOM

Breaking free from bondage doesn't happen overnight. It is an ongoing process. Here are three steps that will help you in that process:

1. IDENTIFY the areas of bondage and sinful behavior.

2. IDENTIFY the lie(s) at the root of that bondage.

3. REPLACE the lie(s) with Truth.

In the final chapters, we'll talk more about how to counter lies with the Truth. But first, take some time to think about those first two steps.

What area(s) of bondage or sinful behavior can you identify in your life? *Example: sexting*

. . . .

. . . .

. . . .

. . . .

. . . .

Every area of bondage or sinful behavior in our lives is rooted in a lie—something we've believed that is not true, according to God's Word. Turn to the table of contents and look through the lies we've addressed in this book. **Identify one or more of those lies (or another one the Lord has shown you) that you realize you have been believing.** (You may want to ask a spiritually mature friend or a mentor to help you see the lie that is influencing your behavior.) *Example: "I need a boyfriend."*

. . . .

. . . .

. . . .

. . . .

. . . .

[lies young women believe]

List any ways in which you have fueled that lie by listening to or dwelling on it. *Example: Spending too much time with my non-Christian, boy-crazy friends and reading teen magazines.*

· ·

· ·

· ·

· ·

· ·

What do you need to do to avoid listening to and dwelling on that lie from now on? *Example: I need to start spending more time with my Christian friends, especially because they've really got it together in waiting for God's timing for the right guy. Today I'm burning my stack of* CosmoGirl*! Maybe I'll invite _____ over to the bonfire!*

· ·

· ·

· ·

· ·

· ·

End your time in this chapter by praying that God would give you grace to take the specific actions you recorded above. Ask Him to begin to release you from the power of any lies you have been believing.

"As he thinks
in his heart,
so is he."

PROVERBS 23:7 NKJV

14

How to Find Freedom from the Lies

Replace lies with the Truth

In the midst of writing this book, there have been times when we have found ourselves believing and acting on some of the very lies we were addressing. One week I (Dannah) set off to New York and holed up in a hotel so I could get some concentrated writing time. What a week it was!

I had such fantastic fellowship with Jesus that I entered into an unplanned partial fast. I'd taken water, fruits, veggies, and granola to snack on. Usually when I'm writing, I take long breaks and find a favorite place to eat meals. Not this week! I was so aware of the Lord's presence that I did not *want* to leave that room for three days. As I worked through the lies on body image, relationships, church, and other issues, I felt a nearness to the Lord that I have not felt in some time. (And, granola never tasted so wonderful!)

As I drove back into my hometown at the end of that time, I was assaulted with thoughts and feelings I had not experienced in years. Each thought pierced to the core of my being.

- *"You're fat."*
- *"You're ugly."*
- *"You have nothing to contribute."*
- *"You're not the real deal, Dannah!"*

Within a matter of hours, I'd plummeted from a great spiritual nearness to the Lord directly to a low that brought back what seemed like every bad emotion and insecurity I've ever felt—and most of them were lies I'd just been encouraging you not to believe about yourself through this book!

Can you identify with having thoughts like that rise up to just crush your spirit? What do you do? I know what I did.

I ran for my Bible. I went straight home and cradled it in my arms as I got on the floor before the God of the universe and asked for His Truth to overcome these lies. I dug into my Bible for specific verses to pray aloud and to write in my prayer journal. I took it a step further by going to a special worship service at my church that evening so my mind and heart could be "washed" with Truth. By the time I went to bed, I no longer felt the heaviness that had come upon me so quickly. I'd been set free.

We want you to experience that kind of freedom. There's only one thing with the power to set you truly free: Truth!

In the last chapter we talked about the first two steps of moving from bondage toward freedom:

1. **Identify the areas of bondage and sinful behavior.**

2. **Identify the lie(s) at the root of that bondage.** Stop fueling those lies by listening to them and dwelling on them.

 Now we come to what may be the most important step in finding true freedom:

3. **Replace the lie(s) with Truth.** That is what I (Dannah) did when I got back home after those days in a hotel in New York, when I was bombarded with lies. I countered the lies with the Truth of God's Word! We have seen this principle powerfully illustrated in many, many lives.

TRUTH SETS YOU FREE!

I (Dannah) recently received a letter from a young woman struggling with a deep, shameful secret that was plaguing her. In spite of her belief that "none of" her friends struggle with this, I seem to get an awful lot of requests to counsel teen girls and women about this one. So, listen in. The letter read:

 I have been up and down with this problem so many times, and I just couldn't find anyone to talk to about it because I know that none of my friends struggle with this. But when I turned about thirteen I had

some real hard struggles with masturbation. I always knew it was wrong, but I felt it was the only way I could be normal with my friends who were already having sex.

Then I got hard core saved and stopped for a long time. I wasn't even struggling with it! I got into your Bible study for a while, and it was so awesome because I was free. But this past year it has just really come back to me. I have told God time and time again that I don't want this, but it's back.

You are the first person I have ever told, so this is really hard for me. I really could use your wisdom in this situation. Thank you for listening!

This young woman knew instinctively that masturbation is not pleasing to the Lord. God designed sex and our sexual responsiveness to be something we enjoy in the context of marriage. While the Bible doesn't give a specific command concerning masturbation, it does forbid sexual activity outside of marriage. Sex was never intended to be a solo activity. And besides, if we're honest, we have to admit that lust—which the Bible does clearly condemn—is almost always connected to masturbation.

TOP TEN
PLACES TO POST
SCRIPTURES
WHEN YOU'RE TRYING TO OVERCOME LIES

10.
Your rearview mirror, if you have a car!

9.
The back cover of your Bible!

8.
Your lunch box, if you're still a packer!

7.
Your best friend's bedroom so she can read them to you!

6.
Your mom's purse, for drastic emergencies!

5.
Your locker!

4.
Your Instagram feed or Facebook page for everyone to see!

3.
Your computer!

2.
Your bathroom mirror!

1.
Beside your bed!

T.R.Y. TO EMBRACE TRUTH

By Amanda Libby, guest blogger on
LiesYoungWomenBelieve.com

Dannah and Nancy mentioned the need to embrace truth. *Embracing truth IS embracing CHRIST!* When we call to Jesus, our minds are redirected toward HIM. Our feelings and emotions may not be there right away, but our decision can be based on the solidity of **God's Word and His Son.**

My mom invented this acrostic of the word *try.* Sometimes we feel like we just need to *try harder* to remember to dwell on truth ... but look at trying this way:

Totally

Relinquishing and

Yielding

Totally relinquishing and yielding ourselves to God is what trying should be. It is essentially *surrender.*

Lies can seem to eat us up, inside and out. But how can we fight them? *Surrender to Jesus!* He will transform those lies to truth. Jesus is greater than lies. He is **Truth. Believe Truth.** *Believe Jesus. Be set free!*

In my response to this young woman, I explained that secrecy is a breeding ground for sin and suggested that she open her heart to an older, wiser friend who could pray for her and encourage her in the battle. I told her that while this battle may not be quickly or easily won—she may fight it off and on for many years—by God's grace this sin *can* be overcome!

As we communicated further, it became apparent that the problem always seemed to increase when she was less connected to God. When she stopped praying, being in Bible study, and reading the Word, she felt strangled by the temptation. When she was first saved and when she was consistently in the Word of God, she experienced less temptation or none at all. Ironic? Not really.

Truth is not merely an idea or philosophy. Truth is a person—the Lord Jesus Christ. He said of Himself, "I am the way, and *the truth,* and the life" (John 14:6). True freedom is found in a vital, growing relationship with the Lord Jesus. He has revealed Himself (the living Word of God) in the Scriptures (the written Word of God). Staying close to both the living and the written Word of God will bring you freedom!

REPLACE THE LIE(S) WITH TRUTH

When we (Dannah and Nancy) find our minds and emotions swirling with things we know are contrary to God's way of thinking, we try to stop and identify the Truth that counters those lies. We're talking about finding specific Scripture verses. We speak the Truth to ourselves—sometimes aloud and, if necessary, over and over again—until the Truth displaces and replaces the lies we have been believing.

For example, I (Nancy) remember being in a meeting in our ministry where some long-simmering issues came to a full boil. One of my coworkers said some things about me that I felt were untrue and extremely damaging. I was devastated.

When I got home that evening, I had a meltdown. All I could think about was how wrong the other person had been and how hurt I felt. I became obsessed with trying to figure out how to vindicate myself. I careened down a spiral of anger and self-pity. I began to believe lies like:

➡ That person *intended* to hurt me.

➡ I deserve better!

➡ It was that person's fault. I am totally innocent!

➡ I cannot forgive them.

➡ The damage cannot be undone.

➡ Our relationship will never be restored.

➡ I have a right to defend myself so others know the truth.

HAVE YOU FELT THE LIES BOMBARD YOU?

Believing those lies resulted in hours of inner turmoil. Have you been there? Are you there now? Have you felt the lies bombard you through a broken relationship where someone has wronged you?

The next morning I opened my Bible and began to read where I had left off the day before. I found myself in the gospel of Matthew. That's where I had a head-on collision with the Truth:

BLESSED ARE THE MEEK . . .
BLESSED ARE THE MERCIFUL,
FOR THEY SHALL RECEIVE MERCY . . .

BLESSED ARE THE PEACEMAKERS . . .
**But I say to you, Do not resist the one who is evil.
But if anyone slaps you on the right cheek,
turn to him the other also. . . . Love your enemies and
pray for those who persecute you . . .**

FOR IF YOU FORGIVE OTHERS THEIR TRESPASSES,
YOUR HEAVENLY FATHER
WILL ALSO FORGIVE YOU, BUT IF YOU
DO NOT FORGIVE OTHERS THEIR
TRESPASSES, NEITHER WILL YOUR FATHER
FORGIVE YOUR TRESPASSES.

(Matthew 5:5, 7, 9, 39, 44; 6:14–15)

Now I had a choice. Would I continue to believe the lies, or would I embrace the Truth? That's when the battle really started. I wanted to nurse the grudge; I wanted to stay angry. I wanted to somehow hurt the person who had hurt me. But in my heart I knew that would only lead to bondage.

I knelt before the Lord, and with the open Bible in front of me, I grappled with the Truth. I knew I had to forgive—that I must release the offender and the offense. I felt there was no way I could forgive, but deep down I knew the issue wasn't that I *couldn't* forgive but that I didn't *want* to forgive.

I knew if I was going to walk in the Truth, I had to relinquish any right to get even or to withhold love from that person. I chose to walk in Truth. My emotions did not change right away, but over the course of the next few weeks God healed my heart and freed me completely.

The discipline of replacing the lies with Truth takes time and commitment. You may need to renew your mind by posting specific verses, memorizing them, and reviewing them regularly, in order to deal with specific areas of bondage in your life. But, oh, the freedom on the other end is worth every bit of effort.

[lies young women believe]

>>> In the next chapter we want to equip you with some **specific truths** that will help you **do battle** against many of the **lies** you may find yourself encountering.

"In Christ and in His Word,
we have the Truth
that sets people free.
That is Good News!"

NANCY DeMOSS WOLGEMUTH
LIES WOMEN BELIEVE

15

The Truth That Sets Us Free

Powerful **Truths** to counter everyday lies

In this final chapter, we want to highlight twenty-two Truths that we believe will radically transform your life if you will choose to believe and embrace them. These are key Truths we find ourselves going back to over and over again.

CAN YOU DO US A FAVOR? Rather than skimming through this chapter, take the time to focus on these liberating, life-changing Truths.

In the days ahead, anytime you realize you are believing lies, go back and review this list. Let the Truth of God begin to replace the lies and renew your mind and heart. Meditating on the Truth will change the way you think, the way you respond, and the way you live!

1 When you're having a **really** bad day and are tempted to feel that God is **not** good

God is good (Psalms 119:68; 136:1). When everything is going just right, it's not hard to believe that God is good. But when you get into a fight with your best friend or are dumped by your boyfriend, the Enemy will move in and cause you to question God's goodness. The Truth is, regardless of your circumstances, regardless of what you feel, God is good, and everything He does is good.

2 When you feel **far from God** and are tempted to feel that He **doesn't** love you

God loves me and wants me to have His best (Romans 8:32, 38–39). God doesn't love us because we're lovable or worthy, but because He is love. There is absolutely nothing we can do to earn or deserve His love. We cannot fully grasp God's unconditional love because no human being can ever love us perfectly or fill the deepest needs of our heart. If we believe God's love is real and receive it, it will transform our lives.

3 When you feel ugly or fat

I am fearfully and wonderfully made (Psalm 139:14). Though you are bound to have a bad hair day now and then, God still considers you His masterpiece. He crafted you just as you are with precision and purpose.

4 When you feel rejected

I am accepted in Christ (Ephesians 1:4–6). You may have been rejected by a parent, a friend, or a boy you liked. But if you are a follower of Christ, you are accepted by God. We don't have to perform to get Him to accept us. Even though we are sinful, we can stand before God clean and totally unashamed, acceptable to Him. How? Because Jesus—the pure, sinless Son of God—is acceptable to Him, and we stand accepted before God through Jesus!

5 When you feel you need more "things" and are consumed by your desires

God is enough (Psalm 23:1). *"The LORD is my shepherd; I shall not want"* (NKJV). You've probably memorized that verse. But have you ever thought about what it means? As a shepherd cares for his sheep, God has promised to meet all the needs of His sheep. The Truth is, if we have Him, we have everything we need.

6 When you feel anxious about your circumstances

God can be trusted (Isaiah 28:16). God keeps His promises. He has promised never to leave or disown us (Hebrews 13:5). He has promised that those who trust in Him will never be disappointed (Psalm 22:5). When you feel fearful or anxious about circumstances or problems, remind yourself that God has never once let anyone down (Psalm 56:3), and He is not going to start now!

[lies young women believe]

7 When you feel like something has happened to you that will ruin your life forever

God doesn't make any mistakes (Isaiah 46:10). Sometimes other people make serious mistakes that affect our lives. But if we belong to Christ, He is holding our lives, and nothing can touch us that has not first been "filtered through His fingers of love." That doesn't mean we won't have problems—we will! But if we will embrace those challenges as being from His hand, He will use them to draw us closer to Himself and to make us more like Jesus.

8 When you feel like you can't handle a problem you're facing

God's grace is enough for me (2 Corinthians 12:9). As children of God, we will never face a problem that is too big for His grace to handle. Even where sin is seeming to run us over, His grace is greater (Romans 5:20). When we are weak, He is strong. When we are empty, He is full. When we have no resources of our own left, His resources are still overflowing! No matter what you are going through right now, His grace is enough.

9 When you feel like your sin is too great for Him to forgive

The blood of Christ is sufficient to cover all my sin (1 John 1:7). There is not a sin you have ever committed or a sin you could ever commit that cannot be forgiven and covered by the all-powerful sacrifice of Jesus' blood. This should not make us take sin more lightly; instead, the understanding that our sin required the blood of the Lord Jesus should give us even greater desire to obey God, by the power of His Holy Spirit who lives in us.

10 When you feel like you'll never be able to overcome a sinful habit

The cross of Christ is sufficient to conquer my sinful flesh (Romans 6:6–7). Through the death of Christ and our relationship with Him, we have been set free from the power of sin. When you do sin, it's not because you couldn't help it, but because you chose to yield to your old master. The Truth is, we do not have to sin, and every sinful pattern in our lives can be overcome by the power of Christ living in us (Romans 6:14).

11 When you feel like your potential is limited by your past

My past does not have to control my future (1 Corinthians 6:9–11; 2 Corinthians 5:17; Philippians 3:12–14). Satan tries to convince us that our past experiences and failures make us worthless, or that we will always have to carry the baggage of our past. But if you are a follower of Jesus Christ, you have been cleansed by the blood of Jesus and set apart for His holy purposes. The Truth is that our past—the ways we have been wronged, and the ways we have wronged others—does not have to be a hindrance. In fact, by God's grace, it can actually become the pathway to greater blessing and spiritual usefulness.

12 When you feel like you don't know where to turn for help and advice

God's Word is sufficient to lead me, teach me, and heal me (Psalms 19:7; 107:20; 119:105). The Word of God is alive and powerful. You can depend on His Word to change your life, deliver you from bondage, and reveal His will for your life. Whatever your need, whatever your circumstances, the Word of God is sufficient to meet that need.

13 When you feel like God is asking you to do something that's impossible

Through the power of His Holy Spirit, God will enable me to do anything He commands me to do (1 Thessalonians 5:24; Philippians 2:13). God does not command us to do anything that He does not give us the grace to do. That means, for example, that

- there is *no one* you cannot love (Matthew 5:44)
- you *can* give thanks in all things (1 Thessalonians 5:18)
- there is *no one* you cannot forgive (Mark 11:25)
- you *can* be sexually pure (1 Thessalonians 4:3–4)
- you *can* honor your parents and respond obediently to their authority, even when you disagree with them or they are imperfect (Ephesians 6:1–3)

By depending on God's grace and the power of His Spirit, we can choose to be obedient, no matter how difficult the command!

14 When you want to **blame others** for your responses

I am responsible before God for my behavior, responses, and choices (Ezekiel 18:19–22). We may not be able to control the things that happen to us, but we can control how we respond to the things God has allowed to come into our lives. When we stop blaming other people and circumstances for sinful behaviors or negative patterns in our lives and begin to assume personal responsibility for our own choices, we will be released from the sense that we are helpless victims. We will be free to obey God regardless of our circumstances.

15 When you are tempted to believe that **your choices today** don't really matter

My choices today will affect my future (Galatians 6:7–8). The choices you make today will have consequences in the future, not only in your own life, but in the lives for those who will come after you. *"Do not be deceived . . . whatever one sows, that will he also reap"* (Galatians 6:7). Every selfish, sinful, or indulgent choice we make today will come back as a harvest in our lives. The harvest is often not immediate. But it will come. The good news is that you are young and you can still make good choices that bring about a good harvest!

16 When you want to **resist an authority** or feel like submitting will steal your freedom

The greatest freedom I can experience is found by submitting to God-ordained authority (Ephesians 5:21). When we resist authority, we become more vulnerable to Satan's attacks and to sin. On the other hand, when we willingly take our place under those God has placed in authority over us, we are granted God's protective covering. We also reveal to the world the beauty of God's created order and proclaim His right to rule over the universe. Best of all, Satan is defeated in his attempts to dethrone God, and we cooperate with God in establishing His kingdom.

17 When you feel like giving up on the church

I need the church (Ephesians 2:19–22; 5:25; 1 Corinthians 12:12–27; Hebrews 10:25). The church matters to God and it should matter to us. Jesus loves the church and died for it. Every child of God is a part of the church, the body of Christ. Every member of the body needs every other member. We were meant to function as a whole body. You might be the hands, or feet, or eyes. We can't function without you filling your role. God's Word encourages us to not stop coming together as the body of Christ. You will grow best in the church, imperfect as it is. Stick it out. It'll be worth it.

18 When you feel that a career is more rewarding and valuable than marriage and motherhood

If God calls me to be a wife and a mom, that is one of the greatest callings in the world (Titus 2:4–5). Marriage and motherhood are God's plan for most women. Young women should rejoice in this calling and prepare themselves to fulfill it if and when God reveals that to be His will for their lives. For a wife and mother, contrary to what our culture says, no career, no hobby, no relationship, no priority is more vital. To make a home, to be united with a man in glorifying God on this earth, to nurture the lives of children and grandchildren, to train and mold the next generation—in the will of God, this is a high and holy calling, with eternal significance.

19 When you are tempted to sacrifice holiness for immediate fulfillment

Personal holiness is more important than immediate happiness (Ephesians 5:26–27). God did not save us just to make us happy in the immediate sense—He saved us to "redeem us from all lawlessness and to purify for himself a people for his own possession who are zealous for good works" (Titus 2:14). The Lord Jesus didn't come down to this earth and die so we could live for ourselves and our own pleasure, but so we could be free to live a life that pleases Him. Pleasing God will sometimes require sacrifices. But any sacrifice we make is temporary and cannot be compared with the joy and fulfillment we will gain in eternity. Only through seeking to be holy can we ever experience true happiness.

20 When you become consumed with **wanting God** to fix your life

God is more concerned about changing me and glorifying Himself than about solving all my immediate problems (Romans 8:29). When life gets hard, our natural instinct is to demand solutions—to find a way out of our problems. If this is our view, we will be tempted to become discouraged and angry when God does not "cooperate" with our agenda. What matters most to God is that we reflect His glory. Some of the problems that frustrate us the most are actually tools He has designed to make us more like Jesus. To demand that He provide a solution or an escape from that impossible situation may cause us to forfeit a higher good that He is seeking to bring about in our lives.

21 When you **don't understand** a difficult situation you're facing

It is impossible to be godly without suffering (2 Corinthians 4:17; 1 Peter 5:10). Suffering takes on a whole new perspective when we realize that it is an essential tool in the hand of God to conform us to the image of Jesus. The process of spiritual growth takes place as we embrace the hard things, rather than running from or resenting them.

22 When you want things to go **your way**

It's not about me; it's all about Him (Colossians 1:16–18; Revelation 4:11)! The world was not created to revolve around us. The entire universe was created to revolve around Christ. If our goal in life is to be happy or accepted or loved, then anything that threatens our well-being will be an enemy—an obstacle to fulfilling our objective. On the other hand, once we agree with God that we exist for His pleasure and His glory, we can accept whatever comes into our lives as part of His sovereign will and purpose. We will not resent, resist, or reject the hard things, but embrace them as "friends," designed by God to make us like Jesus and to bring glory to Himself.

We hope you'll embrace these Truths and hide them in your heart. To help you, we've created a pull-out section for you at the end of the book (see page 213). We'd encourage you to:

Post this list in your bedroom, locker, or somewhere you will see it every day.

<<< V V V

Review these truths—again and again and again; periodically read these truths aloud, until your thinking becomes aligned with God's way of thinking.

Memorize the key Scriptures that correspond to each Truth.

∧ ∧ ∧

Make copies of the list and share it with your friends. Remind each other of specific truths that apply to real-life situations you face.

<<<

"Many deceivers have gone out into the world. . . . Watch yourselves, so that you may not lose what we have worked for, but may win a full reward."

(2 JOHN 7–8)

A Final Word

from Our Hearts to Yours

Remember how we began this book? We asked you to imagine we were sleeping over at your house. In the middle of the night we smelled smoke and heard the crackle of a fire. It was coming from your bedroom door. We promised we wouldn't waste time worrying if it bothered you when we banged on your door and hollered for you to wake up! If you were in a burning house, we would place your safety over your comfort.

Well, we've tried hard to awaken you!

You may have disagreed with our approach from time to time. You may even have been angry at points. Fighting blazing fires can be messy.

But, oh, is it worth it when you save a life!

HOW'S YOUR LIFE LOOKING SINCE WE BEGAN? We hope it's been doused with some of God's refreshing Truth.

God's presence is a refreshing, miraculous flow of living water that you can pour all over the blazing lies that Satan attempts to set roaring through your life. And that flow of living water *is* Jesus Christ. Remember that Truth is not merely an idea or a philosophy, as so many of today's popular worldviews suggest. Truth is a *person*—the Lord Jesus Christ. He said of Himself, "I am the way, and the truth, and the life" (John 14:6). Jesus did not point to a religious system or a code of conduct. He pointed to Himself:

**"If you abide in my word,
you are truly my disciples,
and you will know the truth,
and the truth will set you free. . . .
So if the Son sets you free,
you will be free indeed."**
(John 8:31–32, 36)

Remember: True freedom is found in a vital, growing relationship with Jesus Christ. Jesus (the living Word of God) has revealed Himself in the Scripture (the written Word of God). If we want to know Him, we must devote ourselves to reading, study, and meditation on the written Word. There is no substitute, and there are no shortcuts. The Enemy is constantly confronting us with his lies. In order to combat his deception, our minds and hearts must be filled with the Lord Jesus and saturated with His Word.

BUT IT'S NOT ENOUGH TO KNOW THE TRUTH. We must also
surrender to it. That means we must be willing to change our thinking and our lifestyle in any area that is inconsistent with the Truth as it is revealed in the Word of God.

Millions of teens who claim to be Christians and are active in their youth groups are nonetheless deceived; they are walking in ways that simply are not biblical. Their values, their responses, their relationships, their choices, and their priorities reveal that they have bought into the lies of the Enemy and embraced the world's way of thinking.

Living according to the Truth requires a conscious choice to reject deception and to embrace the Truth. That is why the psalmist prayed,

Remove from me the way of lying,
And grant me Your law graciously.
I have chosen the way of truth.
(Psalm 119:29–30 NKJV).

Would you ask God to deliver you and keep you from any lies that may have lodged themselves in your mind and heart? And would you purpose in your heart to choose "the way of Truth"? That will not always be easy—at times it will be really hard. But the way of Truth is the way of true blessing and joy.

We can't explain this, but we love you. We truly do. We want God to rescue you from the lies of this world.

We want you to embrace life—His Life in you—to the fullest!

We want you to enjoy the freedom He came to give you.

We want your life to fulfill every purpose for which He created you.

And we pray that God will use *your* life to help others in your generation—and the next—experience the great freedom and joy of walking in the Truth!

[lies young women believe]

Log on to our website at:

LiesYoungWomenBelieve.com

This book is just the beginning of the conversation.
We'd love to keep talking about how to identify lies
and replace them with God's Truth!

Join the thousands of girls from around the world
who visit the blog daily to discuss the content of this book,
read about lies that we didn't cover in these pages,
and find a daily dose of God's Truth!

You can also find us on:

Instagram: @LiesYoungWomenBelieve

Twitter: @LYWBblog

Facebook: Lies Young Women Believe

✤ Thanks! ✤

Behind every book is a story of how it came to be. In that story are characters who bring the story to life. We would like to thank those characters in (for the most part) the order they appeared. (Just like the credits that roll at the end of a movie!) *Thank you . . .*

Greg Thornton & the Moody Publishers Team—Greg has worked with both of us for over two decades. We have enormous respect for his wise, godly leadership in our publishing as well as our personal lives. He had the vision for this book and to bring us together back in 2006.

Other, newer members of the Moody team have come alongside us to help out with this revised edition. *Thank you,* Randall Payleitner, Judy Dunagan, Connor Sterchi, Erik Peterson, and others who serve so graciously behind the scenes.

Erin Davis—Erin stepped in as our beloved nationwide discussion group leader when we were originally writing this book. She met with hundreds of girls and surveyed even more to help us really get into your heads and hearts. For this revision, Erin put on the hat of editor. She did a ton of heavy lifting for the book you're holding in your hands right now—how could we ever thank you enough?

Mike Neises & the Revive Our Hearts Staff—Mike blesses Nancy by overseeing the details of her publishing ministry. He invested a great deal of time into the Moody Publishers/Revive Our Hearts/Pure Freedom partnership for this project. Thanks, Mike!

Wolgemuth & Associates—When we first wrote this book, Robert Wolgemuth was my (Nancy's) agent. Since then, he has become my husband. That's an amazing story for another book. (I love you, precious!) And Erik Wolgemuth, what a gift and help you have been in the process of this updated edition.

Jennifer Lyell, a dear friend, was an invaluable part of the original team for this project. During this recent revision, she remained an advisor and prayer warrior.

Friends who served in countless ways—coordinating discussion groups, participating in those groups, doing careful research, reading and commenting on the manuscript, and more. Special thanks to *Jessie Minassian* and *Dree Hogue* for your help in reviewing the original book and providing valuable input and suggestions for this updated edition.

Friends who prayed us through each stage of the process—They held up our hands through the long days and late nights. The Lord heard their prayers and kept refilling us with strength and joy in the journey. The lives that will be affected through this book are the fruit of their love and their faithful labors in prayer.

Bob, Robby & Aleigha, Lexi & Autumn Gresh—Bob has always acted as my (Dannah's) agent as well as the lover of my heart to help me stay confident and focused during this work when, at times, the Enemy sought to make me believe lies I thought I'd long ago overcome. Our children have grown since we first published this book and Robby has brought his dear wife, Aleigha, into our family. As we originally wrote this, they offered lots of advice as teens themselves. Thanks for always supporting this mom of yours.

Jesus—Thank You for knitting our hearts together and for being the Truth that truly has set us free. We love You.

Nancy & Dannah

Chapter 1: The Deceiver

1. "Ten Leading Causes of Death by Age Group, United States – 2014," National Vital Statistics System, National Center for Health Statistics, CDC, https://www.cdc.gov/injury/images/lc-charts/leading_causes_of_death_age_group_2014_1050w760h.gif.

2. http://dictionary.reference.com/browse/lie.

3. "Youth Risk Behavior Surveillance System, https://www.cdc.gov/healthyyouth/data/yrbs/index.htm.

4. Dennis Thompson, "U.S. Teens Less Sweet on Soft Drinks," July 7, 2016, https://consumer.healthday.com/diabetes-information-10/sugar-health-news-644/u-s-teens-less-sweet-on-soft-drinks-712485.html.

5. Tim Elmore, "Responding to Five Trends in Youth Morality (Part 1)", July 22, 2014, http://www.huffingtonpost.com/tim-elmore/responding-to-five-trends_b_5605885.html.

Chapter 2: The Deceived

1. Becky Freeman, *Mom's Everything Book for Daughters* (Grand Rapids: Zondervan, 2002), 29.

2. Ibid, 30.

Chapter 3: The Truth

1. http://dictionary.reference.com/browse/truth.

Chapter 4: Lies about God

1. Christian Smith and Melinda Lundquist Denton, *Soul Searching: The Religious and Spiritual Lives of American Teenagers* (New York: Oxford Univ. Press), 68, 69.

2. "Most teens believe prayers are answered, study finds," http://www.biblicalrecorder.org/content/news/2004/5_13_2004/ne130504bmost.shtml.

Chapter 5: Lies about Satan

1. Timothy Tutt, "The Modern Church Doesn't Need a Make-Believe Devil," https://www.onfaith.co/onfaith/2014/05/15/the-modern-church-doesnt-need-a-make-believe-devil/32086.

2. The book of Job affirms that Satan must have God's permission to harm those who belong to Him. Within the Job narrative, Satan acts at God's directive. Texts like Job 6:4; 7:14; 9:17 point to God as the ultimate decision-maker in whether or not Satan was free to attack Job.

3. In 2 Corinthians 12:7–10, for example, we see that a messenger from Satan was sent to discourage Paul. Satan himself did not do this work.

4. Jeff Hindenach, "Study: Younger Generation Could Be Paying Credit Debt Until They Die," *The Huffington Post,* March 18, 2013.

5. "Pornography Statistics 2003," *Internet Filter Review*, 2004 (12 January 2004). Cited on http://www.family.org/socialissues/A000001155.cfm.

6. David Kinnaman, "Teens and the Supernatural," *Ministry to Mosaics* (Vol. 1) (Ventura, CA: Barna, 2006) 15.

7. http://en.wikipedia.org/wiki/Yoga.

8. Kinnaman, "Teens and the Supernatural," 15.

9. http://biblehub.com/interlinear/galatians/5.htm.

Chapter 6: Lies about Myself

1. Jeff Shewe, "Kate Doesn't Like Photoshop: Digital Ethics," www. photoshopnews.com/2005/04/03/kate-doesn't-like-photoshop/.

2. Bob Smithouser, "They Said It!", *Brio*, July 2007, 15.

3. Jenna Gordreau, "Are Millennials 'Deluded Narcissists'?", January 15, 2013, http://www.forbes.com/sites/jennagoudreau/2013/01/15/are-millennials-deluded-narcissists/#7b277ce35ac2.

4. The American Freshman: National Norms Fall 2016, https://heri.ucla.edu/.

5. Kevin Eagan et. al., "The American Freshman: National Norms Fall 2015", https://www.heri.ucla.edu/monographs/TheAmericanFreshman2015.pdf.

Chapter 7: Lies About Sexuality

1. https://www.blueletterbible.org/lang/lexicon/lexicon.cfm?strongs=1&t=KJV.

2. *The MacArthur Study Bible* (Nashville: Word), Song of Solomon 3:5.

3. Dr. Joe McIlhaney, *"Building Healthy Futures"* (Austin, TX: Medical Institute for Sexual Health, 2000), 25.

4. Robert T. Michael, John H. Gagnon, Edward O. Laumann, and Gina Kolata, *Sex in America* (New York: Warner Books, 1995), 124, 125.

5. Debbi Farr Baker, "SDSU Study: Sex for Women Is Earlier, with Less Guilt," *San Diego Union Tribune*, October 4, 2005. (Citing a study from the San Diego State University.)

6. Richard Leonard, *Movies That Matter: Reading Film through the Lens of Faith* (Chicago: Loyola Press, 2006), 47.

Chapter 8: Lies about Relationships

1. Suzy Weibel, *Secret Diary Unlocked: My Struggle to Like Me* (Chicago: Moody, 2007), 16, 52.

2. Michael Gurian, *The Wonder of Girls: Understanding the Hidden Nature of Our Daughters* (New York: Atria Books, 2003), 128.

Chapter 9: Lies about My Faith

1. Joe Neill, "Staying Power When the Door Looks Soooo Good," http://www. youthspecialties.com/articles/topics/power/staying.php.

2. *American Heritage Dictionary.*

3. Libby Lovelace, "Lifeway Examines Teenagers' Views on How to Get to Heaven," Lifeway.com, May 2007.

Chapter 10: Lies about Sin

1. Nancy Leigh DeMoss, *Brokenness: The Heart God Revives* (Chicago: Moody, 2005), 143.

2. "Texting While Driving," https://en.wikipedia.org/wiki/Texting_while_driving.

3. Erin Schumaker, "10 Statistics That Capture the Dangers of Texting and Driving," July 7, 2015, http://www.huffingtonpost.com/2015/06/08/dangers-of-texting-and-driving-statistics_n_7537710.html.

Chapter 11: Lies about Media

1. Lauren E. Sherman et. al., "The Power of the *Like* in Adolescence," May 31, 2016, http://journals.sagepub.com/doi/abs/10.1177/0956797616645673.

2. Bob Smithouser, *Movie Nights For Teens* (Chicago: Tyndale, 2005), 2.

3. Ibid., 2.

4. Ibid., 1. Quoting Stephen King from *Entertainment Weekly*, November 2003.

5. R. W. White, "Self-Concept in School Adjustment," *Personnel and Guidance Journal*, vol. 46, 1976, 478–81.

Chapter 12: Lies about the Future

1. Ted Olsen, ed., "Go Figure," *Christianity Today*, June 2007, 16.

2. "Letters to the Editor," *People*, July 2, 2007, 8.

Chapter 13: How to Stop Fueling the Lies

1. Beth Moore, *Feathers from My Nest* (Nashville: Broadman & Holman Publishers, 2001), 156.

POST THIS LIST
in your bedroom, locker,
or somewhere you
will see it every day.

Overcoming Lies with the Truth

✢ **WHEN I'm having a really bad day and am tempted to feel that God is not good. God is good.** • "Give thanks to the Lord, for he is good." Psalm 136:1

✢ **WHEN I feel far from God and am tempted to feel that He doesn't love me. God loves me and wants me to have His best.** • "For I am sure that neither death nor life, nor angels nor rulers, nor things present nor things to come, nor powers, nor height nor depth, nor anything else in all creation, will be able to separate us from the love of God in Christ Jesus our Lord." Romans 8:38–39.

✢ **WHEN I feel ugly or fat. God created me as a masterpiece.** • "I praise you, for I am fearfully and wonderfully made. Wonderful are your works; my soul knows it very well." Psalm 139:14

✢ **WHEN I feel rejected. God accepts me through Christ.** • "He chose us in him before the foundation of the world, that we should be holy and blameless before him. In love he predestined us for adoption to himself as sons through Jesus Christ, according to the purpose of his will, to the praise of his glorious grace, with which he has blessed us in the Beloved." Ephesians 1:4–6.

✢ **WHEN I feel I need more "things" and am consumed by my desires. God is enough.** • "The Lord is my shepherd; I shall not want." Psalm 23:1 • "Keep your life free from love of money, and be content with what you have, for he has said, 'I will never leave you nor forsake you.'" Hebrews 13:5

✢ **WHEN I feel anxious about my circumstances. God can be trusted.** • "Commit your way to the Lord; trust in him, and he will act." Psalm 37:5

✢ **WHEN I feel like something has happened to me that will ruin my life forever. God doesn't make any mistakes.** • "This God—his way is perfect; the word of the Lord proves true; he is a shield for all those who take refuge in him." Psalm 18:30 • "The Lord will fulfill his purpose for me; your steadfast love, O Lord, endures forever." Psalm 138:8

✢ **WHEN I feel like I can't handle a problem I'm facing. God's grace is enough for me.** • "But he said to me, 'My grace is sufficient for you, for my power is made perfect in weakness.' Therefore I will boast all the more gladly of my weaknesses, so that the power of Christ may rest upon me." 2 Corinthians 12:9

✢ **WHEN I feel like my sin is too great to be forgiven. The blood of Christ is sufficient to cover all my sin.** • "But if we walk in the light, as he is in the light, we have fellowship with one another, and the blood of Jesus his Son cleanses us from all sin." 1 John 1:7

✢ **WHEN I feel like I'll never be able to overcome a sinful habit. The cross of Christ is sufficient to cover my sinful flesh.** • "We know that our old self was crucified with him in order that the body of sin might be brought to nothing, so that we would no longer be enslaved to sin. For one who has died has been set free from sin." Romans 6:6–7

✢ **WHEN I feel like my potential is limited by my past. My past does not have to control my future.** • "Therefore, if anyone is in Christ, he is a new creation. The old has passed away; behold, the new has come." 2 Corinthians 5:17

✢ **WHEN I feel like I don't know where to turn for help and advice. God's Word is sufficient to lead me, teach me, and heal me.** • "The law of the Lord is perfect, reviving the soul; the testimony of the Lord is sure, making wise the simple." Psalm 19:7 • "He sent out his word and healed them, and delivered them from their destruction." Psalm 107:20 • "Your word is a lamp to my feet and a light to my path." Psalm 119:105

WHEN I feel like God is asking me to do something that's impossible. Through the power of His Holy Spirit, God will enable me to do anything He commands me to do. • "He who calls you is faithful; he will surely do it." 1 Thessalonians 5:24. • "I can do all things through him who strengthens me." Philippians 4:13

WHEN I want to blame others for my responses. I am responsible before God for my behavior, responses, and choices. • "The soul who sins shall die. The son shall not suffer for the iniquity of the father, nor the father suffer for the iniquity of the son. The righteousness of the righteous shall be upon himself, and the wickedness of the wicked shall be upon himself." Ezekiel 18:20

WHEN I feel that my choices today don't really matter. My choices today will affect my future. • "Do not be deceived: God is not mocked, for whatever one sows, that will he also reap. For the one who sows to his own flesh will from the flesh reap corruption, but the one who sows to the Spirit will from the Spirit reap eternal life." Galatians 6:7–8.

WHEN I feel that submitting to an authority will steal my freedom. The greatest freedom I can experience is found by submitting to God-ordained authority. • "Remind them to be submissive to rulers and authorities, to be obedient, to be ready for every good work." Titus 3:1

WHEN I feel like giving up on the church. I need the church. • "As it is, there are many parts, yet one body. The eye cannot say to the hand, 'I have no need of you,' nor again the head to the feet, 'I have no need of you. . . .' That there may be no division in the body, but that the members may have the same care for one another." 1 Corinthians 12:20–21, 25 • "Not neglecting to meet together, as is the habit of some, but encouraging one another, and all the more as you see the Day drawing near." Hebrews 10:25

WHEN I feel that a career is more rewarding and valuable than marriage and motherhood. God's Word highly values the roles of marriage and motherhood. • "And so train the young women to love their husbands and children, to be self-controlled, pure, working at home, kind, and submissive to their own husbands, that the word of God may not be reviled." Titus 2:4–5

WHEN I am tempted to sacrifice holiness for immediate fulfillment. Personal holiness is more important than immediate happiness. • "[Christ] gave himself for us to redeem us from all lawlessness and to purify for himself a people for his own possession who are zealous for good works." Titus 2:14

WHEN I become consumed with wanting God to fix my life. God is more concerned about changing me and glorifying Himself than about solving my problems. • "Even as he chose us in him before the foundation of the world, that we should be holy and blameless before him. In love he predestined us for adoption to himself as sons through Jesus Christ, according to the purpose of his will, to the praise of his glorious grace, with which he has blessed us in the Beloved." Ephesians 1:4–6 • "Now may the God of peace himself sanctify you completely, and may your whole spirit and soul and body be kept blameless at the coming of our Lord Jesus Christ." 1 Thessalonians 5:23

WHEN I don't understand a difficult situation I'm facing. It is impossible to be godly without suffering. • "And after you have suffered a little while, the God of all grace, who has called you to his eternal glory in Christ, will himself restore, confirm, strengthen, and establish you." 1 Peter 5:10

WHEN I want things to go my way. It's not about me; it's about Him. • "For from him and through him and to him are all things. To him be glory forever. Amen." Romans 11:36

"[We] have no greater joy
than to hear that [you] are
walking in the truth."

(3 JOHN 4)

Revive Our Hearts™

Through its various outreaches and the teaching ministry of Nancy DeMoss Wolgemuth, *Revive Our Hearts* is calling women around the world to freedom, fullness, and fruitfulness in Christ.

Offering sound, biblical teaching and encouragement for women through . . .

 Books & Resources Nancy's books, True Woman Books, and a wide range of audio/video

 Broadcasting Two daily, nationally syndicated broadcasts (*Revive Our Hearts* and *Seeking Him*) reaching over one million listeners a week

 Events & Training True Woman Conferences and events designed to equip women's ministry leaders and pastors' wives

 Internet ReviveOurHearts.com, TrueWoman.com, and LiesYoungWomenBelieve.com; daily blogs, and a large, searchable collection of electronic resources for women in every season of life

Believing God for a grassroots movement of authentic revival and biblical womanhood . . .

Encouraging women to:

- Discover and embrace God's design and mission for their lives.
- Reflect the beauty and heart of Jesus Christ to their world.
- Intentionally pass on the baton of truth to the next generation.
- Pray earnestly for an outpouring of God's Spirit in their families, churches, nation, and world.

Visit us at **ReviveOurHearts.com.** We'd love to hear from you!

"Every time I read this blog it is exactly what I need."
– LiesYoungWomenBelieve.com blog reader

You KNOW you're set free by God's Truth . . .
but sometimes you still feel challenged
by the deceiver's lies.

Join a community of young women like you, who are
journeying together to seek and choose Truth. Read
powerful posts by our team of bloggers and be encouraged and challenged to dig deep into Scripture.

LiesYoungWomenBelieve.com

Go Deeper.
Expose the Lies with Truth.

The truth may not change your circumstances, but it will change you.

THE TRUTH WILL SET YOU FREE

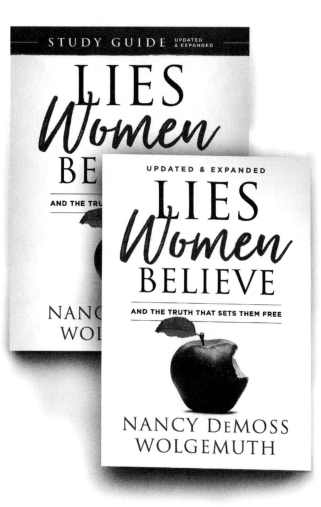

Lies Women Believe has sold over one million copies. Now, in an updated and expanded version, Nancy DeMoss Wolgemuth shares this liberating message with a new generation, spotlighting forty-five lies commonly believed by Christian women. It offers the only means to challenge, counter, and overcome deception—the Truth.

Go online for more
lie-breaking resources

Explore more books helping readers counter
lies with the Truth, please visit

LIESBOOKS.COM

The Power of Modesty for Tweens!

Abstinence isn't about **not** having sex— it's about waiting to have it **right**.

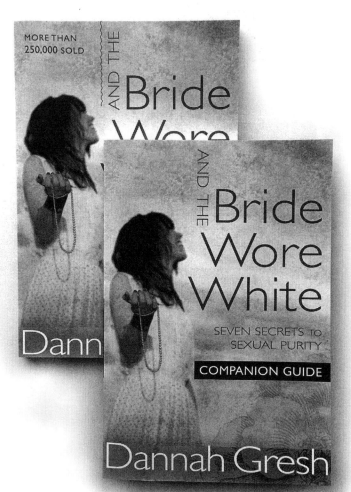

Bestselling author Dannah Gresh exposes Satan's lies about sex, gives a three-step plan to breaking off sinful relationships, and provides compassionate guidelines for healing. Since its release in 2000, *And the Bride Wore White* has impacted the lives of hundreds of thousands of young women.

BOOK 978-0-8024-1258-4 | **ALSO AVAILABLE AS AN EBOOK**

COMPANION GUIDE 978-0-8024-9400-9